HERMIAS
IPPOCRATOUS 59,
ATHENS, 106 80
TEL. 3641121
FAX. 3619641

**Popi Panagis**

# A Journey to Crete

**HERMIAS**

Library of Congress catalog number : 208-256
Published in Greece by Hermias Publishing House

**The author manages to make the land and the people of the Greek island of Crete speak to us in the language of the heart. The stories in this book are radiant with the courage, humor, and determination of a people tried by war and misfortune. The author reveals to us the close interconnection of the land that bore them and the geography of the spirit that shaped them.**

**Stephen Bacigal**
**Editor, SAY WHAT!**
**(Greek - American Union)**

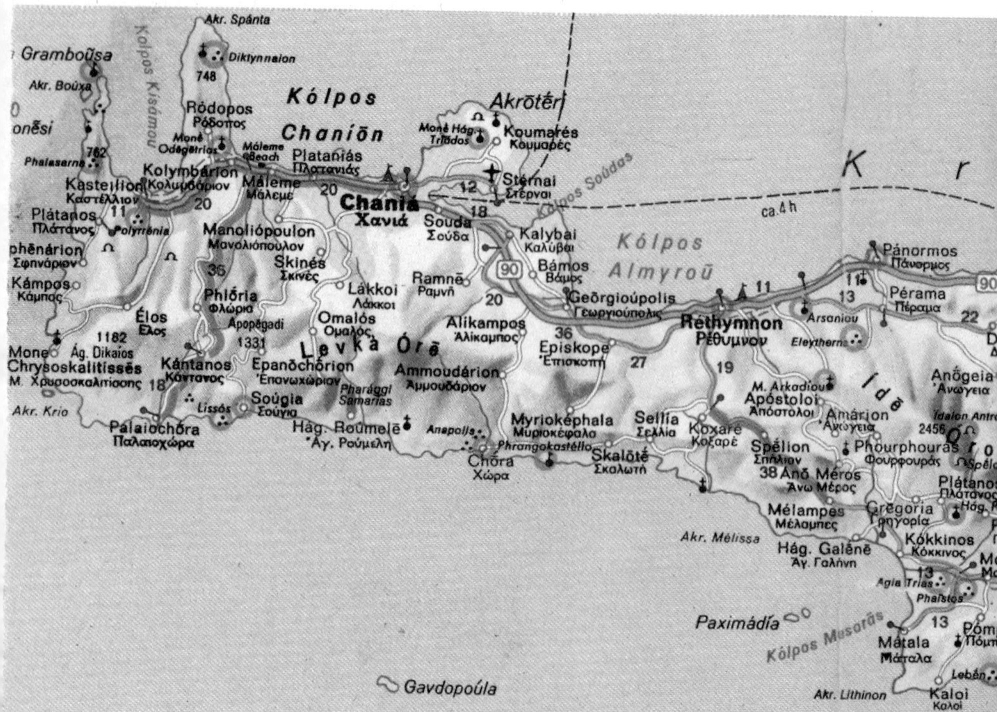
Akr. Spánta
Gramboũsa
Diktynnaion
748
Kolpos Kisámou
Akr. Boũxa
Kólpos
Akrōtẽri
Rodopos
Ρόδοπος
Chaníōn
Koumarés
Κουμαρές
Monẽ Hag. Triádos
Monẽ Odēgẽtrias
Máleme Beach
Phalasarna
762
Plataniás
Πλατανιάς
Kolymbárion
Κολυμβάριον
Kasteilion
Καστέλλιον
Máleme
Μάλεμε
20
Stérnai
Στέρναι
Kólpos Soũdas
K r
Chaniá
Χανιά
12
18
Plátanos
Πλάτανος
11
Polyrrēnia
Manoliópoulon
Μανολιόπουλον
Souda
Σούδα
Kalybai
Καλύβαι
ca. 4 h
Kólpos
Almyroũ
Pánormos
Πάνορμος
phẽnárion
Σφηνάριον
Skinés
Σκινές
36
Bámos
Βάμος
90
Kámpos
Κάμπος
Ramnẽ
Ραμνή
Lakkoi
Λάκκοι
Phlõria
Φλώρια
Geõrgioúpolis
Γεωργιούπολις
11
13
Pérama
Πέραμα
Élos
Έλος
1182
Apopẽgadi
Omalós
Ομαλός
Alikampos
Αλίκαμπος
Réthymnon
Ρέθυμνον
Arsaniou
22
Mone
Ág. Dikaios
Chrysoskalitíssẽs
Μ. Χρυσοσκαλιτίσσης
1331
Levka Órẽ
Episkopẽ
Επισκοπή
27
Eleytherna
Kántanos
Κάντανος
18
Epanõchõrion
Επανωχώριον
Ammoudárion
Αμμουδάριον
19
Anõgeia
Ανώγεια
M. Arkadiou
Apóstoloi
Απόστολοι
Idẽ
Akr. Krio
Lissós
Soúgia
Σούγια
Pharággi Samarias
Myrioképhala
Μυριοκέφαλα
Sellía
Σελλία
Amárion
Palaiochõra
Παλαιοχώρα
Hág. Roũmelẽ
Άγ. Ρούμελη
Anapolis
Koxarẽ
Κοξαρέ
2456
Phrangokastéllo
Skalõtẽ
Σκαλωτή
Spẽlion
Σπήλαιον
Phourphouras
Φουρφουράς
Chõra
Χώρα
38
Anõ Méros
Άνω Μέρος
Plátanos
Πλάτανος
Mélampes
Μέλαμπες
Gregoria
Γρηγορία
Akr. Mélissa
Hág. Galẽnẽ
Άγ. Γαλήνη
Kókkinos
Κόκκινος
13
Agia Trias
Phaistos
Paximádía
Kólpos Musarãs
13
Mátala
Μάταλα
Gavdopoúla
Akr. Lithinon
Lebẽn
Kaloi
Καλοί

Dία
Akr. Stavrós
Hērákleion
Ηράκλειον
Knōssós
Κνωσσός
Amnisós
Goúrnai
Γούρναι
Limēn Chersonēsou
Λιμήν Χερσονήσου
Soūblos
Σούβλος
Akr. Hág. Iōánnēs
Brouchās
Βρουχάς
Kólpos
Merampéllou
Dragonáda
Gianysáda
Akr. Sideros
Élasa
Chersonēsos
Χερσόνησος
Mália
Μάλια
Dréros
Epánō Eloūnta
Επάνω Ελούντα
Neápolis
Νεάπολις
Krásion
Κράσιον
Kastéllion
Καστέλλιον
Epánō Archánai
Επάνω Αρχάναι
Lyttos
Tzermiádon
Τζερμιάδον
Éxō Potamoí
Έξω Ποταμοί
Hág Nikólaos
Αγ Νικόλαος
Pseíra
Skopē
Σκοπή
M. Toploū
Seteia
Σητεία
Baion
Phoinikodasos
Akr. Pláka
Palaikastron
Παλαίκαστρον
Mardátion
Μαρδάτιον
Móchlos
Shaka
Σφάκα
Piskoképhalon
Πισκοκέφαλον
Diktē
Óre
Antron
Lasithion
Latō
Kritsá
Κριτσά
Bathýpetron
Βαθύπετρον
Arkalochōrion
Αρκαλοχώριον
Kaboúsion
Καβούσιον
Ornón
1237
Praisos
Zákros
Ζάκρος
Káto Zákros
Κάτω Ζάκρος
Hág. Barbára
Αγ. Βαρβάρα
Panagia
Παναγία
2148
Mālai
Μάλαι
Kalòn Chōrion
Καλόν Χωρίον
Gournia
Pacheiá Ammos
Παχειά Άμμος
Ziros
Ζίρος
Tephélion
Τεφέλιον
Amirās
Αμιράς
Anatolē
Ανατολή
Lithinai
Λιθίναι
Kalòn Chōrion
Καλόν Χωρίον
Kastéllion
Teménē
Favriána
Demati
Gdóchia
Γδόχια
Phérma
Φέρμα
Makrygialós
Μακρυγιαλός
Gra-Lugiá
Γρα Λυγιά
Hierápetra
Ιεράπετρα
Mesochōrion
Μεσοχώριον
Achentrias
Tsoutsouras
Loūrai
Λούραι
Pýrgos
Πύργος
Keratókampos
Κερατόκαμπος
M. Arbēs
Mýrtos
Μύρτος
Akr. Goudoūra
Kouphonēsion
Kóphinas
1231

## TABLE OF CONTENTS


**SECTION 1**
PREFACE
Author's Introduction 13
Crete's Historical Background 21

DISCOVERING THE ISLAND
The Cretan Civilization 25
Crete and Its Beauty 30
Going to the Sea Under the Shadows 41

**SECTION 2**
BASIL'S STORY

**CHAPTER 1**
LIFE AT THE BEGINNING OF THE WAR 51
The Goats 59
The Lost German 61

**CHAPTER 2**
THE ROLE OF THE RESISTANCE IN CRETE 65

**CHAPTER 3**
BEGINNING OF THE RESISTANCE MOVEMENT 73

**CHAPTER 4**
THE MISSIONS 81
Taking a Swim 85
In German's Boots 95
The Trap 97
Striptease 100
A Drink of Water Just in Time 102
The Great Potato Hunt 105

**CHAPTER 5**
ESCAPE OF THE ITALIAN MAJOR CARTA 115

**CHAPTER 6**
THE RESISTANCE SPREADS 121
**CHAPTER 7**
THE FORMING OF THE 'GESTABITES' SECURITY FORCE 131

**CHAPTER 8**
AFTER THE ABDUCTION OF KREIPER 137
The Burning of Anogia 140
Running for Death 143

**CHAPTER 9**
FUNNY AND PECULIAR INCIDENTS
DURING THE RESISTANCE 145
The Beggars 145
The Monk's Hole 148
Going for Snails 150
Digging for Salt 153
The Boy With the Supper 154
The Battle of the Pig 158
The Boy With the Rifle 159
The Runaway Horse 160
The Surprise Encounter 162
The Mistaken Victim 164
The Guide Manolio 166

**CHAPTER 10**
THE AMERICAN 171
Beginning of the End 177
The Sixteen Prisoners 179

**CHAPTER 11**
THE GERMAN RETREAT 183
The Parting 189

**EPILOGUE**
The Outrageous 195
The Unexpected Striptease 195
The Surprise Meeting 196
Author's Epilogue 197
**Bibliography** 199

# SECTION ONE

# PREFACE

# DISCOVERING THE ISLAND

## AUTHOR'S INTRODUCTION

*At every place we visit we want to know about its ancient history. Why don't we consider its modern history? After all, recent history is the direct link between us and the past. Furthermore, it is easier to identify with the recent past and understand the conditions, the circumstances, the chain of events that provoked the actions that challenged the established order and posed threats to liberty and justice. We would know how these threats came about, what provoked them and sustained them under similar conditions. This knowledge would enable us to be prepared and deflect any threats to our liberty.*

*We should learn from the previous generation first hand their trials and adventures that can make reality fiction, or fiction reality, not just the historical events as they are recorded in books, but human tolerance and ingenuity in carrying the burdens of war, the human drama that is carried in the absurdity of war.*

*My quest took me to Crete, to an island of Greece, to my native land, to discover that experience, to learn first hand the trials and adventures of the people there... about the outrageous and impossible during the second world war; not only to discover and learn from their war experience, but also to discover their land, their island of beauty that is like a jewel in the Aegean Sea. Their island as being my roots from my father's side of the family, stood in my dreams as a land of a destination some day, to explore and see its natural beauty, and learn about its history, and its people with their traditions, customs, and legends: their way of life.*

*What a better way to start than to go there to mingle with the people and take part in one of the most celebrated of rituals: a wedding.*

*After a long trip, I, my daughters, my mother – my husband had to stay behind – and my 'Koumbari', a Cretan couple going to Crete to get married of which I was going to be maid of honour, arrived in Crete.*

*First, let me more fully explain the term 'Koumbari'. It is a unique, Greek social norm, that has a meaning which goes beyond the significance and obligations that all of us know are included with being the best man or the maid of honour in a wedding. In Greek custom the relationship of 'Koumbari' marks the beginning of the bond with the newlyweds, as their 'koumbari' will be their closest and honoured friend throughout the couple's lives. Furthermore, there is a specific term for men: 'Koumbaro' and for women: 'Koumbara' whereas 'Koumbari' includes all. The same relationship is extended in baptising children too. In baptising children the 'Koumbari' will be like second parents in protecting and loving the child.*

*Why am I explaining this? Why am I going into detail to explain specific social Greek norms. Well, even though I'm of Greek nationality, I consider myself as 'Greek-American,' in a way, because I have been fortunate to live equally in two cultures. I say fortunate, for my life was enriched with knowing the fabric of two societies, and compare them, hopefully to get the best of them, the best of human experience to guide my life. It gave me that extra spectrum to write this book, to write this story, bringing the elements of the setting of the story, the characters, the true events, with empathy, with understanding. To bring to the surface the story with the understanding of one who lived in that culture, and having that extra spectrum to communicate all, with enough sensitivity, all those concepts in a different language of one's own.*

*Of course, the process was long and painstaking. As English wasn't my native language I have had to put a lot of effort in learning it... to the consternation of my husband and children. Can I blame them? Since they have had to stumble over books in every room of the house - even in the bathrooms - or even late at night while studying for tests, my husband would say, "Come on, turn off the light, you have to get some sleep. I have to get some sleep too. I can't, knowing that you're up too."*

*They understood, I couldn't do any different. Imagine somebody learning the alphabet at a later stage of life. It was like going to the kindergarten again.*

*At that time I lived in California. Between having children and working I reached college where I got my first degree. I remember all my family were present at my graduation. They must have been one of the noisiest at the ceremony.*

*They would point at me, "Here is mommy," and my eldest daughter kept saying: "Do I have to be married and have kids to finish college? Is that how long it takes?"*

*Afterwards we moved from California to Alaska where I started taking courses again to continue my education, to reach the 'impossible dream' of mine: to be a writer someday - I had to plan for the time when my children leave home, and materialize what best represents myself, writing. Anyhow I continued taking courses until one summer, I took an oral history class just before going to Crete, with my 'koumbari,' to marry them (na tous stefanoso) which in Greek means that during the ceremony the 'Koumbari' act, or almost are in equal footing with the priest in exchanging the couple's vows, as the rings, and also according to Greek custom, to hold and exchange two small wreaths over the heads of the couple. At a marriage ceremony the priest represents heaven; 'koumbari' symbolises mankind, and united in purpose, they represent heaven and mankind joining together to consecrate the sacred union of marriage.*

*Finally we approached the end of the journey. As we neared Crete's port of Heraklion, the island seemed to me like an old world entering a new age. I gazed at a brilliant sky surrounding the island, and covering the port's Venetian castle. A magic pull from that ancient harbour took me from reality and I almost expected Venetian war warriors to come out and defend their fort.*

*The closer I approached the more I was able to relate to reality as I saw tanned lean figures exuding resoluteness, strolling by or at the foot of the castle. They wore either modern outfits or the traditional garb of Cretan 'vrakes' (pantaloons) with distinguished jackets. Oh well, I thought, I went back in centuries for a minute.*

*When inland, and going on our destination, to our 'koumbaro's village, my Cretan experience began. The whole island began to unfold before my eyes as to leave me in amazement. I was deeply impressed by the island's vastness and contrasts while climbing switchback roads through rugged mountains and driving close to the edge of abysses, observing the ample valleys, some low, as if in the depths of the earth itself, and others towering.*

*"Eh! 'koumbara', you see, I told you. Going through Crete's mountains and valleys is an adventure," my 'koumbaro' said sensing my amazement as I looked around grasping the configuration of the high peaks of the mountains and the openness of the valleys.*

*It was nightfall when we neared the village Aghio Mama, which stood out white against the darkness... As we approached the village the sound of a characteristic tune broke the night's silence. Climbing out of our vehicle, we stepped on the stone ground in the yard of the house. Flowers in arrays around the edge of the patio and set on a higher level, completed a picture of the terraced patio covered with grape vines. Flowers touched us like feathers, people greeted us with warm, strong handshakes, others sat around tables or danced hand in hand in circles. Some whirled and leaped to the music. Their feet were a joy to watch, the complicated steps of the Cretan 'pendozali' dance were mesmerizing.*

*"Where are we, on Broadway? We should take pictures," I said.*

*"There's not enough film in my camera," my youngest daughter answered.*

*"Your forgetting to load our camera has become a legend," my oldest snapped back.*

*"But not the same legends as we have here in Crete," said a Cretan next to us.*

*"What kind of legends?" I asked.*

*"Ancient kings and gods, living there."*

*"Where?"*

*"In the mountains..." the Cretan continued, as he pointed to a gigantic outline of the mountains in the distance.*

*People came forward, "Come on 'koumbara', dance!"*

*Hands clapped, faces expressing full enjoyment gave approval.*

*"Opah," (go, go). Glasses clinked to toasts of 'Is Iyia' (to health) then... gunfire.*

*Oh no, I thought. What's going on... unless the Germans are coming again; I was influenced by my all encompassing thoughts about my oral history project here in Crete.*

*"Are the Germans coming again? Why are you shooting? I said in amusement as I tried to enact a scene of my potential project.*

*"Koumbara, they came, they saw, they destroyed, but they did not conquer."*

*Who would dare? I couldn't help thinking when I saw guns laying on the laps on some young people. Even a machine gun was set by a window.*

*Shots were going out in the air through the windows of the house.*

*My mother, who had never seen a gun before and forgetting that she was among friends, was so shocked for the first minutes that she shouted out... "Oh! my gosh, are these guns real? Help! help!.."*

*"Don't be afraid 'Koumbara'. We aren't!" said some women trying to comfort her.*

*"Take a look at this one," one of the young men said putting a gun on my mother's lap.*

*"Take it away from me. It's real," my mother shouted again, "guns at weddings?"*

*It was a wedding pre-reception.*

*"We Cretans celebrate life's big events with such passion that the danger of death has lost its meaning for us," said the young man.*

*"Like in the war," I said.*

*"Eh, 'syntekne', (meaning 'fellow family man') remember how... when*

*the Germans came..." said a voice in strict Cretan dialect.*

*He spoke for a few minutes about some incidents, episodes, about getting smart with the Germans during the war and also who was who in the resistance.*

*My search started right there!*

*I had to find and interview someone who had taken a leading role in the resistance. Somebody who was behind the scenes at the beginning of the war but who advanced later in the resistance's command structure; somebody who would be typically Cretan in his character.*

*I finally found the person. A man who had not taken any credit, or had not wanted to take any credit. One of the real heroes who is in such harmony with himself that he doesn't need the validation of other people, but only to fill a purpose in life, to leave a mark in life. After I talked to numerous people in many villages and towns I found the person in the city of Heraklion, where he lives to this day in an apartment just a few minutes walk from the Venetian castle by the sea. From there he can get a taste of the sea by going fishing, as he can get embraced by the mountains when going to his village to take care of his land.*

*His apartment was not hard to find. A short marble staircase led up to a well-kept apartment building, which contrasted in style with its neighbouring older city houses. I entered and immediately felt the coolness of the shade. Further up the stairway my eyes fell on a lush row of plants which were carefully lined up. It was like taking a breath of cool air in the hotness of the day. I couldn't avoid following the plant line which took me to his door.*

*The plants, tropical plants, plants with colorful leaves - red, fuscia - or plants with small flowers ready to open, extended into the house as far as the balconies, creating an oasis in a concrete desert. As the breeze which swept through the balconies moved the plants' leaves, the plants displayed a motion as if they were about to take a sail, I imagined, over the rooftops and away from the city.*

*The house exuded a certain kind of homely coziness accentuated by elaborately crafted Cretan furniture.*

*Surrounded by wall photos and tables covered with impressive hand-embroidered tablecloths displaying artifacts, was Basil. He greeted me with such dignity with such honour that I can only label it Cretan. Looking at his pictures I remember what I was told about him: "Basil was not only entrusted with secretly keeping safe gold used by the resistance but after war's end he received a medal for his war deeds."*

*'Yes, indeed,' I thought, 'an unpretentious person,' as I looked*

*around for but couldn't see, a picture of him being awarded a medal. Only later when he showed me his war pictures was I shown it. It was quietly kept in a drawer.*

*The interviews took place in the afternoons. His tall, lean, stalwart figure in the semi-lit room, looked larger in life, a challenge to life as his tanned face, long with strong futures, framed decisive eyes set under distinguished brows. From his solid resonant voice, his story... or incidents he heard from other people, unfolded with passion.*

*Every afternoon for many days, I sat hearing stories about the war, but not from a historical point of view. I was seeking a point of view of personal experience of the war, under oppression, the absurdity of war. How was everyday life under such conditions, how did ordinary people cope, in their struggle? What was their contribution to the outcome of the war in recent times, not just the events, but the incidents, the circumstances, the coincidences what composes the web of life under such conditions? How were the blows of war managed?*

*Basil would recall these details, others he would not want to talk about, yet other details would be sketchy because from a man's point of view they were not important to be mentioned. Clearly they were important enough to be retained, so those memories in order to be brought out needed some prodding, an intense, from every angle questioning from me, in order to elicit responses about every side of an event. Basil allowed me to complement what he couldn't verbalize, to fill out what he said in scanty details.*

*Then, in translating and writing the story, I had to interpret what his statements implied, in vivid detail and to enact the scenes, to make dramatizations, to elicit characterizations, to bring out not only the gist of every incident, but also everything that underlay it, as in the incident, 'The Great Potato Hunt'. Thus, in a sense I was writing the story.*

*He agreed for the release of his memoirs only for my college project, but did not want them to be published.*

*"It would be of no use," he said, "What I did, I did it for a cause, for my country."*

*I respected his wish, and after I translated and used some parts for my project I set it aside for a few years. Then certain events in my life demanded that I draw inspiration from the story, from the people of the story, the way they coped, the way they used their own resources, the way they challenged the circumstances which spelled there is no way out. Their attitude under such extreme and severe conditions became lessons for me, when they had to cope with life's ultimate threats: destruction, terror and death.*

*All this made me question over and over what Basil said of not wanting to have his story published.*

*"It would be of no use," he would say.*

*But yes there is. How can a younger generation build its ideals, or rally courage when it has no contemporary role models, true heroes, to identify with and to derive inspiration? How can we dare to take chances, to challenge life to the ultimate, to challenge the circumstances that say there is no way out? If we don't hear the stories of others who did and how they got through under similar circumstances of our present societal conditions, how can we have the assurance that the 'impossible' can be done. Why leave a vacuum and not make a connection with a recent past that tells us who we are, and what mental and physical resources we have inherited? We are endowed with our environment. We should protect it and not allow others to destroy it. How can we overcome the difficulties of the present if we don't stand on the foundation of the gains of our recent past? And above all it shows us for what we should strive for.*

*He agreed.*

*Out of respect for his privacy, because he didn't want his story to be published in the first place, I'm not disclosing his complete name, but I'm revealing as much as I can about a real person, a real character, who can be found.*

## CRETE'S HISTORICAL BACKGROUND

During my research, I found out that although the Cretans' own contributions were enormous, there is little mention of them in history books, if any at all. Thus, after interviewing different people I compiled this personal account of war adventures as told to me by someone who took one of the leading roles in the resistance. Cretan resistance was perhaps the most effective of the war and was certainly the most unusual. This uniqueness was due to Crete's location.

The island of Crete lies far south of the Greek mainland and is the island which lay closest to the African battlefront. It was a pivotal location for the Germans, who used Crete as a base for reinforcements sent to the Middle East.

Little did the Germans know that all their mechanical means would stumble on the resoluteness of the local people to hinder the Axis powers from one of their plans, to reach and take hold of the rich oil fields. The Germans were already fighting in Africa and urgently needed Crete as their base. The Cretans demonstrated their resoluteness and resistance from the very start which was at the Battle of Crete, when the Germans attacked with paratroopers in what was the first airborne battle in history.

When the paratroopers removed their parachutes upon landing, they had to face an adversary who was ready to fight to the end. These Cretan fighters, elderly men, young boys and women fought with makeshift weapons, side by side with the remnants of the remaining allied forces, for days in strategic points of the island.

The whole island was a battlefield as all the people there were defending their land, but the odds were steeply stacked against the Cretans because the Cretan division was absent fighting at the northern border of Greece. Only after the Germans sent more paratroopers, more reinforcements, and many bombers, were they able to invade the island.

The German losses were enormous as the battle of Crete delayed them from making headway on other battle fronts.

According to a German Major who took part in the battle, the battle was unusual. "...The Cretans lay in wait for us behind every tree, every house, every bush, shooting from every hiding place and combating the German soldiers."

After the Battle of Crete the people hindered the Germans by creating an effective local resistance network although no one had any prior training in military or espionage tactics. Using only human resources, these ordinary citizens supported the underground fighters in the long struggle against the Nazis, supporting them even to the point of sacrificing their own lives and lifeblood to this noble cause.

Those resources used to render the enemy war machine impotent were ingenuity, friendship, cooperation, dedication, sacrifice, persistance and humility. During the occupation following the Battle of Crete, Cretans supported and hid allied soldiers who fought that battle. These soldiers fled to the southern part of the island until the allied ships were able to rescue them.

The resistance network was vitally important to the allies and formed the backbone of the ally efforts to frustrate the advance of General Rommel in the Middle East. The only way the allies could halt Rommel was to stop reinforcements from reaching him. Rommel's reinforcements came from the closest German supply base located between Europe and the Middle East, the island of Crete. Crete became Rommel's transit camp. Without Crete, Rommel couldn't have made those advantages in such a short time. With the people's passive resistance, and their cooperation in the destroying of air bases from where the reinforcements originated, the allies were they able to solidify and organize their position to counterattack on other fronts, as to change the whole course of war.

The Cretan people's accomplishments were performed with boldness, devotion and humility. Their heroism is revealed in the stories that follow, but their humility is best illustrated by the narrator himself. We can see these qualities, his modesty, and the pure devotion of his personality emerge through these episodes and through him we can see the character of the Cretan people he represents.

Although this story takes place during World War II and is based on historical facts, it is not told from a historians' perspective. This story is told from the point of view of the common people whose experience of the war, through their missions and expeditions, included both humour and horror.

We see this juxtaposition of emotions in many episodes such as the one titled 'The Beggars'. What makes the story so unusual and captivating is that it is full of episodes where different ironic, comic, and chance events interact, demonstrating the complexity and absurdity of life's everyday circumstances.

These stories indicate that perhaps war is not what we think it is the enemy, the weapons, the premeditated strategic plans, the superior military might that can overcome everything. Perhaps war is the battle of life to survive, to accomplish and to move forward.

## THE CRETAN CIVILIZATION

The Cretans are the descendants of Minoans, a prehistoric advanced society. The Minoans were the first civilization in Europe that ruled commerce in the ancient world, administrated ancient laws, produced fine artifacts and built great palaces as early as 2000 B.C. They were named after their king, Minos, who established a dynasty comparable only to that of the pharaohs in Egypt.

While Europe was in a primitive stage, the Cretans were building their advanced society, showing a great sense of justice in society and beauty in the arts. They ruled their marine empire including the Greek islands of Cyclades, Peloponesos and part Sicily from their first organized royal navy in history. Five magnificent palaces in Knossos provided the seat of government, and also a center of storing grains in silos, tucked away in a multitude of storerooms.

Their religious life was influenced by the cycle of nature and the seasons of the year which determined growth. Their life in the palace was among bullfights and processions, dances and plays. These could be viewed as the forms of sports, religion and theater.

The palace walls are adorned with magnificent frescoes and murals depicting religious or social scenes. One such fresco depicts bold scenes in a bull ring with acrobatics done by matadors, far more dangerous than any modern matador would dare. Landscapes animated with either animal or fish, and displaying maritime life, compliment this Cretan art.

Evidence that women played a major role in Cretan civilization is shown by a temple fresco scene on the palace walls showing a crowd of five hundred ladies, who were partaking in these Cretan festivities. Furthermore, a statue of the snake goddess, a trim female figure with the arms and upper parts of the body covered with snakes, has been found which according to ancient norms, symbolizes god-like qualities.

Other indications are seen in the murals, on which a double axe symbol, believed to be a symbol of femininity, has often been placed.

Murals depicting bull scenes and cult festivals express the

creativity of the Cretan artist. The themes of these murals show the sincere depth of their love of life, through a combination of grace and originality.

The original palace in Knossos is resting in the midst of a group of low rolling hills. It was reconstructed in our century by Sir Arthur Evans, the English archeologist who discovered the site and unearthed remains of the civilization, hidden for four thousand years.

The royal buildings, the theater, the courtyards, the staircases, and the shrines all create the great magnitude of the site. These variations in structure, with the asymmetrical layout of the building, allowed for the reconstruction of the site that was also necessary to preserve the theatrical staircases and the throne room. The throne, an intricately carved piece of art, is the oldest one in Europe.

The feeling of experiencing something grand begins right when you enter the site. First, you enter an apparently ceremonial corridor that bears works of art and leads you to a magnificent view of the mountains and the sea; then, you head towards a great central court from where a maze of the structures extend and descend on various levels.

In the buildings, reconstructed ornate columns supporting the roofs and lining stairwells, accentuate the solidity and solemnity of the structures. Stairs lead you underground to the queen's chambers decorated with flying dolphins. Also underground is the famous labyrinth which held the legendary in Cretan history, Minotaur, a creature half human and half bull.

The labyrinth is a maze of corridors in an intricate and tortuous arrangement. You can go through this maze but only to a certain point, and always following directions, otherwise you are bound to get lost.

Evans gave the palaces visual effects, by creating light wells. air shafts, and water drainage systems. These additions made the site more captivating by giving an extra measure of realism, while enhancing its original glory by presenting a long glorified past coming slowly to life.

Close to Heraklion at Mallia is another cluster of Minoan palaces. The structure of the Mallia palaces is similar to the ones in Knossos – as the ancient remains reveal – with sacral rooms, storerooms and royal apartments. These palaces though don't have the luxurious tones, the decorations, and the richness of Knossos, but they exude an air of mysticism; on the courtyard there is the famous 'Kernos', a round stone different than any other. The stone is dented with evenly-spaced small hollows around the edge and with a large hollow in the centre. There are many interpretations of what it symbolizes, even to a point that it has been a sacrificial stone. If you see it, you can then formulate your own interpretation of what it represents.

The other cluster of palaces, the summer palaces that the rulers used, were in Phaestos located farther south facing the Libyan Sea. Even though Phaestos has not been reconstructed, it remains in fact spellbound to see. What it lacks in architecture and buildings it makes up for in its surroundings. In its simplicity it breathes dignity and peacefulness, that is accentuated with a harmony of sounds, like the rustle of the leaves in the wind, or the singing of the birds in the nearby foliage of olive trees.

The palaces in Phaestos today have only foundations of different plot shapes. As those foundations are sitting on a solitary hill, overlooking the rich fertile plain of Messara, a vast field of trees and plants or grape vines, you can only supply with your imagination what they were like. In fact, it is not only the endless view of the rich Messara plain that engulfs you, it's the panorama of the mountains in the north and south. The proud mountain vistas with the glistening sea at their feet, comprise a harmonious marriage of the land and the sea.

You will feel the grandeur, particularly if you had visited the Knossos palaces before you go to Phaestos. If you arrive at sunset in Phaestos you will see the Messara fields as an interplay of lights and colours of the earth and the sky, reddish purple sunlight bathed in the earth's browns and greens, and if you are lucky, all these while an eagle soars.

Then, when it's dark you relive the grandeur by imagining sitting under a grandiose Knossos-like staircase under the silver moonlight reflecting over the far glistening sea. Now you're a part of history, you are in the pages of history as you see the shadows of these ancient remains on the solitary hill with the beauty of the plain unfolding at a gradual incline to the sea. You can't help thinking that this ancient palace still rules the land as you visualize how it once was.

After a glamorous night, you're fresh in the morning to continue your adventure through these wonders of the natural and ancient world. The road on the southern coast can lead you to another Minoan summer site that has remains of Minoan structures, and is close to the village of Matala, with its natural harbor and its steep cliffs.

The remains are not only ancient Minoan, but sophisticated Roman and Christian as well. The Roman empire engulfed the Cretan civilization temporarily after the Minoan civilization came to an end from a combination of external and internal factors as the coming of the Dorians, other Greeks from the northern part of Greece, who occupied the island. The external forces were the waves caused by an earthquake on a nearby island of Santorini, and that was when, it is believed, the continent of Atlantis disappeared. These factors made the Cretans began the tradition of resorting to the mountains, and becoming known as Eteocretans.

While under the Romans there was an interaction of cultures that allowed for the impressive remains of temples, a Roman theater and a vast underground cistern found in Gorthys that was another capital center of the Roman empire. You get impressed by the setting of the theater as imprinted on one wall is the law code of Gorthys, an ancient text of laws on civil matters. The text, about thirty feet long, with seventeen thousand characters in ancient Greek dialect, reads backwards. The remains surrounded by rough, ancient trees create an atmosphere recalling the grandeur of this period. Walking along the fields you slowly discover each aspect of this engaging site. Crumbled walls, foundations, columns, statues, arches and different fragments exposed, not in any defined order with excavations still in progress, seem to drag other fragments to the surface, to resurrect the ancient Roman empire; next you could imagine Roman chariots marching between them.

After the Roman Empire was the transition period. This was the time when the Arabs turned the island into a pirate's nest until Crete entered a new phase, between the fifth and seventh centuries when the Cretan culture was revitalized under the influence of early Christians. The early Christians left a wide mark in the countryside as the remains of forty impressive basilicas attest. The one remain that stands out is the Basilica of Aghios Titos (Saint Titos) the first bishop of Gortys assigned by Saint Paul to convert the Cretans. The basilica dates from the sixth century and today faint fragments of frescoes are still visible on the walls. An extension of the basilica, a small side chapel, is still used today as a shrine.

The period after the early Christians again was interrupted by Islamic insurgence on the island at times until the fifteenth century when the aggressive missionary activity brought the Venetians who colonized and feudalized the island. The Cretans revolted successfully against the Venetians and were then given equal footing with them. In this period was the development of Creto-Venetian culture that absorbed influence from the west. Poets playwrights, musicians, and painters comprised the Cretan Renaissance. It was then that the Cretan poet Kornaros wrote the epic romance Erotokritos.

The painters instituted such techniques that created the Cretan School of Arts. Painters such as M. Damaskinos and Domenikos Theotokopoulos, or El Greco as he was more known, with their econographies influenced Cretan art for generations. El Greco, who lived in Spain for many years, shows in his paintings a degree of Westernization even though the dominant characteristics in his intricate econographies are of Cretan Byzantine origin.

The Venetians left a dominant mark in architecture. The finest Venetian fortresses, buildings with ramparts, bastions, or columns with decorated carvings, were erected. The enormity of the Cretan countryside, the mountains, the valleys, and the sea contrast with the romantic settings of the Venetian structures. These structures enrich the Cretan landscape in the towns and in the villages as they add an aura of romanticism to the local architecture. In the cities, as Heraklion, Chania, and Rethymnon, are Venetian churches, minuscule palaces, apartment houses with handsome doorways and curved balcony railings, that display the characteristics of that period. In the villages are manor houses and ramparts, remains of Venetian fortresses.

After the Venetians, the Turks entered the scene. The Cretans put up a brave front and only after a sixteen year seige (1650-1666) – one of a kind in history -- in the seige of 'Handaka', the area of an ancient Venetian castle, the Turks were then able to penetrate the island, but only after the Ottoman Empire engulfed Crete with all its might. Eventually, the Cretans accomplished the impossible again, by repelling another conqueror, and by the end of the eighteenth century, Crete regained its autonomy with its own currency, postage stamps and costumes until 1913, when it was finally annexed to the mainland of Greece.

As in the past, the Cretans of today are taking leadership roles in all aspects of cultural and political life, and in European Community affairs. In the field of Arts, a prominent Cretan figure is the author Nick Kazanzakis. He expressed an authentic, dynamic character in his novel 'Zorba the Greek' later made into a movie, starring Antony Quinn. Also there is the Oscar winning composer Manolis Hatzidakis.

The Cretans still show their resolve and independence, while holding to their traditions, but blending to our modern world, accomplishing the impossible, as during the last war. Needless to say the Cretan character is merged with friendliness and hospitality that leaves the visitor with long lasting impression of warmth. This shows the traditional Greek hospitality 'phyloxenia'(love of foreign visitors) as you venture deep into the island's towns and villages.

When entering a Cretan village or town, you are greeted by people expressing inquisitiveness blended with respect. If a wedding procession or other festivity is going on they would want to be your host, to take part in the festivities. They would offer you the plentiful festive food and invite you to their dances and even to show you how to dance the Cretan way, no matter how lost you feel in the intricate dance steps. They would keep encouraging you to dance even though you drag along the way, but you would still feel part of their celebration as you tried to dance with them... or more likely to leap like them. The beat of the music, the swirling of the dancing and saying at the same time 'Opah' (go, go) and you will be following before you know it. Grateful to your efforts at attempting to fit in they would offer food and pure homemade drinks, while trying to make you comfortable: an unforgettable experience for sure.

**Crete and Its Beauty**

Crete lies within a triangle of Europe, Asia and Africa. The island is surrounded by different seas, the Aegean, the Cretan, and the Libyan Sea.

The most distinctive part that played the biggest role in Crete's history are its mountains. They form a tremendous ridge that seems to dissect the island, offering surprising views of mountain vistas. The unexpected views are due to the position of the island as it is where Europe and Africa meets, offering landscapes of contrasting physiology; for example, one side of the mountain slopes can be rugged while the other can be full of greenery.

The range of mountains drops precipitously on the south parts of the island and into the Libyan Sea making the southern coast rugged and not as populated as the northern coast.

This ridge drops gently into the northern coast as it forms sandy stretches of beaches, coves, and natural harbors. This has meant that the habitation is concentrated on the north coast around and behind the coastal areas of Kasteli, Souda, and around the big seaport cities of Chania, Rethymno, and Heraklion. By contrast the southern coast cannot support much of the population and there is only one main town, Ierapetra. Only the large and fertile plain of Messara is close to the south coast.

The mountains have a rugged grandeur and comprise the backbone of the island. They are like making a stance as they are in constant presence, no matter where you are. That grandeur is also revealed in colouring. The mountains take on a characteristic reddish purple tone at sunset, similar to the grandeur of Arizona's Grand Canyon. The skies take that unusual red and purple tone due to the island's proximity to a tropic zone. Sharp contrasts in humidity crystallize the vapor coming from the sea reflecting the fading sunset. In the evening the sky takes a low shading of sienna or ochre colour adding to a dreamy atmosphere.

The southern part of the mountains, having the distinctive feature of being rugged, played a big role during the resistance. They housed the resistance fighters and enabled them to move into unapproachable and formidable territory they knew but the enemy didn't. The enemy, intimidated by the nature of this part of the country, declared it a 'dead zone', only having set military outposts along the coast.

Even though from afar the snowy glittering peaks seem to form a smooth unbroken chain, the mountain ridge is not continuous, for it is broken up into a number of massive peaks. Some of the mountain ranges, such as the White Mountains reveal a mystic quality comparable to the Himalayas. They are called White Mountains because they emit a certain brilliant whiteness, even when there is no snow. When they're enshrouded in layers of mists, they seem to change their appearance from hour to hour and from one minute to the next. The upper heights, with their protruding brilliant peaks, as they are veiled in mists... will bewitch you .

The climate and position is responsible for the island's tremendous variety of wild plants and flowers. The climate is favorable because Crete is generally dry and warm without extremes. Rain or snow vary widely throughout the island, being heavy in certain mountainous areas and light in others. The prevailing north wind can be strong and cool even in the summer. The favorable climate brings an abundance of diversified produce of grains, vegetables and fruits; for example, olives, grapes, carobs, bananas, melons, and peaches on the lower warmer regions and potatoes, onions, and apples on the higher cooler regions. Interspersed with the dominant olive trees are stands of forest trees such as pine, oak, cypress and chestnut, which compliment the diversified landscape.

A prime cultivated plant is the vine. The vine gives varieties of grapes that are used in three ways; the rosaki that is a favoured table grape; the sultana that is used for making raisins; and other varieties that are used for making wines. A favorite liquor from grapes is the famous, pure and fiery 'raki'. The villagers prepare it in traditional ways out in the countryside in secluded huts. The drink is every visitor's welcome treat, and it's served in small glasses on embroidery-covered trays. It's clear and pure to delight the senses, but not to drug them.

The changes of climate affected by the various weather conditions of the mountain heights throughout the year bring lush vegetation of wild spiky plants, shrubs, herbs, and wild flowers in uncountable variety and colours according to season. As you go through the island you would see alongside the roads, plants in different forms according to climatic situations. In fairly damp spots a huge plant 'Agave americana' in different lengths up to twenty feet or more, with rough sharp pointed leaves bearing heads of greenish flowers appear to overcome the roadside. In contrast, on dry spots, a low plant 'Mandrake,' with wrinkled leaves and blue flowers, seem to be overcome by the countryside. The plant appears to be shrinking when its pulled up, hence it's conceptualized as a plant having aphrodisiac properties. In addition, a thorn bush resplendent with minute golden yellow flowers, springs up on rare mountain sites.

Springtime is an explosion of wild flowers. Hundreds of blossoming varieties are everywhere as they conquer the landscape, the mountains, the plains, and the gorges. One hundred varieties of orchids even in rare yellow varieties, are found in abundance in the spring. There are small pink gladioli in the Omalos Plain and on scrubby hillsides are rock roses. Dispersed among the other flowers is the iris with a distinctive orange stripe on its blue flower making an unusual note. Anemones of bright colours give life to a bare ground and a change of pace as they spring up between olive trees that dominate the island.

The wild flowers intermingled with herbs, in different shapes and forms projecting the colours of the spectrum, cover hillsides and plains like velvet carpets let out ready to touch, to comfort and engulf any tired traveler, any exhausted body. The touch, the sight, and the smell of the wild flowers and herbs can amaze the traveler, as they engrave a long lasting impression of the spectrum. The luxurious shades of wild orchids and light rose blossoms serve as an inspiration found in traditional Cretan embroideries and woven handiwork as handbags, rugs, and blankets in intricate classical designs.

This abundant varied plant life, set in a rich spectrum of the earth's colours and textures, attract the bird species and a varied wild animal life, such as the wild goat. The Cretan wild goat known as 'agrimi', may weigh up to 45 kilos and the distance between its horns is up to 78 centimetres; this size doesn't hinder the goat's swift movements as it runs fast, giving the impression of dominating the island. There are many resident and immigrant birds, from the tiny species such as the warble and gold finch to larger species such as the heron, falcon, egret and the golden eagle. Vast numbers of birds migrating between Europe and Africa make stops in Crete enriching the overall habitat of the island.

Most of the mountains are made of limestone set on schist, phyllile or crystalline beds. The mountains are filled with caves that offer spectacular views and romantic images of stalagmites and stalactites in chambers of complicated passages. The caves were used by the Islanders as dwellings, for refuge in times of crises, and as religious shrines. They were the places where ancient myths, legends, and ancient gods were born. One such cave is the birthplace of Zeus, the King of the ancient Greek gods. The cave, one thousand meters in depth and twenty kilometers in length, is set on a rim of the Lasithi Plain. The cave attracted pilgrims and settlers throughout the centuries. Fossil remains of human and animal life, along with artifacts and implements such as pottery and knives, helped to piece the island's history. Climbing to the cave is strenuous but thrilling. You take a winding path through clumps of wild scrubs and oak trees. At the very moment you approach it you can't help but feel overcome by the sacredness of some sort of shrine.

By the cave, the sight of a wild fig tree, the ancient symbol of fertility, along with the sounds of the foliage from the nearby trees, evokes the mysteries of the legends surrounding the birth of Zeus. According to legends, godlike youths, the Currets, covered the cries of the infant Zeus with their dancing and clashing of their swords to the rhythm of the dance. It is said that the fast paced, elaborate Cretan dances seeming to project godlike qualities of sensuality and maleness, descended from the Currets.

As you enter the cave, a muted light from the entrance follows you. The farther you descend into the earth's depth, the more mysterious and sacred the atmosphere. Scrambling first to a vast damp chamber, you're overcome by the vastness of the translucent stalagmites and stalactites. Stalagmites from the floor thrust upward, extending the vital force of the earth to meet the stalactites which are hung from above to become one with them in a dynamic union.

Then, slipping through an opening by a pool of water, you are at the inner sanctum at the actual site of the birth. An aura of comfort and serenity enfolds you as you're surrounded by the colours of childhood innocence, rosy pink colours glowing in rock formations all around the area of the birth.

In the heart of the cave by the sacred pool, the translucent colours and muted light cast shadows giving the illusion of nymphs who would come down to feed Zeus, as in the legend... Time stands still, you are in other times, you are in other dimensions, buried in the earth's insides, all born in the earth's vital insides...

Up to mountain heights are gorges and ravines, 'faragia', where the resistance forces would traverse during the occupation. The most notable gorge is the Samarian, one of the biggest in Europe, some 6,000 feet deep. It was formed by the upheavals of land and the swirling effect of the water. At the heart of the mountains is where you begin descending. Amid circling hills all of the sudden everything falls under you, and a chasm opens wider and wider in tremendous dimensions, more than you expect. Farther down you are confronted by many flowers and greenery, and you may even get a glimpse of the elusive Cretan wild goat.

Passing the chapel of Saint Nicholas, you arrive at the Venetian church of Ossia Maria (saint Maria) the same name given to the gorge.

The church dates from the fourteenth century and has intriguing frescoes on its walls. After passing some stone huts you are deep in the gorge's labyrinth. A river forms and either you can follow it, or go along the upper trails over shrubs and herbs. In the abrupt rock slopes, you might see some people hanging there gathering the herb 'dictanos' that is believed to give sexual agility.

As you plunge in a zigzag trail amid cypress trees, forming different levels of slant lines on the rugged slopes, you would feel the vastness of the gorge. It seems to have become haunted... the different angles of land, plants, trees with the different diffusion of light.. all of the sudden you could picture the natural deities coming into play... nymphs and spirits take you in circles and accompany your descent. In reality what accompanies you is the frothing water coming out from pebbles or gushing springs. Appearing in your way to the bottom of the gorge are olive groves, cypress and chestnut trees, creating a picture of peaceful nature.

Then, everything narrows leading to 'sedoroportes' (iron gates). The atmosphere changes and a sense of the supernatural is at the gates, reinforcing legends of ancient gods or goddesses being born there... like the daughter of Zeus the Cretan Artemis, or the wife of Apollo. Finally, with a sudden drop to the shore you lead your way to the end of the gorge, out to the sea... an abrupt descent out to the real world.

Bordering the gorge is another wilderness area, Sphakia. It is a mountainous stronghold whose inhabitants through the centuries repelled any invader. The people there live according to their long held traditions and with their genuine manner and haughty attitude, they show a proudness that can be interpreted as a challenge to our modern world. Up to-today, they oppose anybody who dares to put any infringements on their territory, to a point to be notorious for their feuds. They work on the land they love by tending flocks or hunting game.

Crete has four principal mountain ranges. At the far east are the Sitia Mountains, and west of these are the Lasithi Mountains; then, over central Crete is the Psiloritis range, the highest mountain at eight thousand fifty-eight feet, also known as the Idha range. In the west are the dominant White Mountains (Lefka Ori). Mount Idha is more rugged than the White Mountains and has many of the same qualities as the White Mountains such as the blue reflection of the sky and the view of the land. From the twisting mountain roads, you can see a panorama of the entire island that is set in motion by the clear, blue water beating on masses of protruding earth - in depth, in breadth, in height, in every dimension. Reflecting the brilliance of the surrounding nature the White Mountains appear a range upon range of shades of bluish white. Looking more closely, you can see that the mountains are constituted with protruding grey and white stones and as they're mixed with the earth's copper and greens they give out a total picture of a perfect blending of the sky and the sea, over earth's immense depths.

The Idha Mountains, like the White Mountains, plunge from their uppermost pinnacles straight into the immense depths of the Libyan Sea in a series of sharp cliffs. From these mountains, the evening begins when the sun sinks into the island, Gathos, radiating the sky with a palette of purples and reds. It's beautiful to see the sun basking momentarily in the horizon and then disappearing as darkness sets in. Between those ranges are green valleys and white villages on the lower flanks, while high above, like clouds, the zig-zag snowy peaks of the Mountains float.

Among the white villages in Psyloritis Mountains is the village of our story Anogia. A twisting road leads you into a rugged landscape of mountains with clumps of wild vegetation that are looming and towering in front of you, as if trying to intimidate and discourage you from going on.

Suddenly, whiteness blinds you. After a sharp bend on the road, you see the village. There, clinging from the roadside are imposing traditional white stone houses separated by twisting paths climbing the mountainside. The houses with their blue designed wooden windows and doors, and with their square little balconies full of attractive flower pots, are inviting, but most inviting are the different stores displaying a plethora, a thesaurus of arts and crafts made with a imaginative skill and care from the village women who learned their skill through the generations.

Hand woven, hand loomed and embroidered tablecloths, pillows, handbags, furniture covers, knick-knacks, rugs, blankets, in classical historical designs, or designs inspired from the Cretan nature, make a dynamic presence. The natural materials used like lambswool, flax, or silk, with their colours, their texture, capture an image of a homely atmosphere of human warmth spilling over objects, making them come alive with care and love, to fill a household with serenity and contentment.

Proud, strong Cretan figures in traditional pantaloons, high boots, and headbands in a slant, walk defiantly like soldiers in uniforms. You can't help but be impressed by this show of pride from these simple village people in their brave wear. This village wear gives an image of strength, a stronghold of unity amongst them.

Above Anogia the road leads towards the Nida plateau where the Idaean cave is located. Historical findings such as Roman coins, bronze shields, and spears attest to the existence of human life there for 5,000 years. The cave is covered with thick snow even in the summer and has a moist, slippery environment. The history, the location, and the environment of the cave gave rise to different legends.

As you go up, you would see dispersed over the countryside, at different heights, over barren, rugged or green slopes, many thorny bushes and spiky plants, hence the high boots worn by the mountain men.

Going further up on the mountains you would enjoy a wide view of Crete... and you might meet some shepherds, who true to their reputation of hospitality, may offer you a drink of their 'raki'.

After passing through rich countryside, by the mountains, along the western flank of mountain Idha, where you can see not only oaks and firs but lush greenery of olives and walnut trees or vineyards, you are in the Amari Valley, which was a centre of underground activity during the war. Being there now in peacetime, you're impressed when you see fields of rippling wheat or fields of trees like cherries, set in levels forming colourful patches in lush green meadows. Complimenting the picture are many villages scattered through the valley around a circular route.

Taking the road to the mountains and viewing the unending mountain vistas of different heights forming a labyrinth of hills, crevices and spasms, you are at the heart of Crete; you hear the musical sound of the sheep bells and the harsh voice of shaggy booted shepherds yelling at their flocks as they round them up. The shepherds being tall, lean, and hearty, and cloaked in sheep skin are moving around with a certain lofty stride, projecting an aura that is a challenge to their surroundings, a challenge to the environment.

Next, you would think you hear an imaginary tune... that is coming from a lyre, their organ they use for their music to accompany the beat of one of their dances 'pentozali'. This means semantically, dance to a climax, dance to a point of dizziness or to exhaustion to bring out all the vital forces locked within you, to disperse them, to diffuse them and to blend them with the environment and feel one with the environment.

Moving further up you would see shepherds gathering around a fire, eating their staple, yogurt, which is made in their huts in the old, primitive way...they are waving at you, inviting you to join them.

With a car or a motorbike you can wander off the main roads, into the villages and up into the mountains where you may find yourself engulfed in Cretan hospitality, a certain warmth, as it is expressed in Greek "Phyloxenia" (love of foreigners). No matter where you are, you would feel the intensity and the vigor of the Cretan character, the Cretan personality as it is expressed in all facets of life. You can see the Cretan showing a passion of life, of nature, while toiling over the land, or while shearing sheep. You can see that same spirit on the Cretan while he is walking on the roads with a certain stride and grace, speaking with liveliness, taking an immense interest in the surroundings, the sunset, the environment, all part of his nature, his very being.

You can see that character moving and dancing proudly with vigor to the distinguished sounds of the lyre, to its distinct beats, breathing new life into you. The elements of the Cretan character is best expressed in the lyrics of their songs, and especially in their 'rizitika' ballads, as the "rizitika" express the authenticity of the Cretan character: defiance, laughing at the inevitable fate of war, and death, or committing acts of courage...

"On a clear day I'm going down from the mountains to the valley to fight the enemy...

"To see the leader riding a horse, surrounded by his men...

"To see how shots are thrown...

"Even though death is dragging me, I'll come, my love, to say the final goodby..."

Or, mocking fate's ugly face, and instead rejoicing, celebrating toasting to the feast of life..

"Time ruins beauty
and youth looses strength,
Only the strong feelings of sorrow
or merriment remains.
Everything gets ruined
Live it up!
With merriment
go against death with obstinacy!

Only that kind of character can express a boldness, an intuitive daring in the flurries or enjoyments of life, in every facet of life, accomplishing the outrageous and the impossible.

Other lyrics expressing a philosophical, even a satirical point of view, to the conditions of life are the 'mantinades'; lyrics sung by one person with impromptu verses made up along the way as each other person, or a whole chorus, slowly responds giving creative smart answers.

Continuing the long chain of mountains to the east, which help to form the backbone of Crete are the Lasithi or Lasiotika Mountains, where resistance movements took place. In addition there are the Asterousia Mountains which separate the Messara plain from the south coast. The Messara plain is at sea level, about twenty miles long and some three miles wide. It is on an east west axis towards the central part of Crete, just up from the south coast, and it is rich and fertile, contrasting with the surrounding mountains. The rugged mountains of Psyloriti, Asterousia, or Lassiotika, can amaze you as they offer a kind of landscape of a different world, of another space... a confusing maze of craters, pits, and chasms encircling rims of plains or valleys.

At the foot of the mountains are huge upland plateaus, basin-like terrain, and the way they are set they appear to be supporting the surrounding slopes. These plateaus are fertile farmland that draw precipitation from the surrounding slopes. Their richness and fertility of their landscape, their variety of plant life, their trees bearing blossoms, and especially their unusual position at different elevations, like huge saucers lying on huge contoured masses of land add to their spectacular views.

Enclosed by a ring of mountains are the big Lasithi plain below

Mount Dikti, at the elevation of 3,000 feet, and the Omalos plain in the White Mountains. The Omalos plain is a mountainous country where shepherds inhabit stone huts in the summer and migrate down to villages during the winter.

The biggest and the most famous is the Lasithi plain. On this upland plateau you would think you were in the depths of the continent. The view is most spectacular at a point where the road bends revealing a plain where in the spring you can see a patchwork pattern of field orchards contrasting with the ruggedness of the surrounding mountains. The plateau is dotted with thousands and thousands of flowerlike windmills turning in the breeze, about ten thousand, the largest concentration of windmills in Europe. Water, in little currents and streams, gushing from nearby springs, journeys across the plain and irrigates the gardens.

Something else is revealed through the mountains. Coming into view and forming a rim above the plain are the eighteen villages of Lasithi. These were proud strongholds of determined people perched up there to view any invaders and repel them as they did throughout Crete's history.

The mountains have shaped the independent character of the people by isolating various settlements at different stages throughout history, and by giving them shelter in times of trouble. The Cretans have adapted to the environment and through generations have learned about every mountain, every valley, every plain, and every path, everything that comprised the surrounding nature, as to give them a strong framework on which their civilization survived through the ages, repelling any conquer, accomplishing the impossible.

Most of the villages in Crete are on different elevations on mountain slopes, or they are dispersed at the edges of the valleys and quite a few are on the waterfront. The mountain villages as they are perched on the slopes along with wayside shrines, form a distinctive part of the Cretan scenery, creating a background view fit for any painting. At night they seem to sway in the dark like floating islands and as the villages' whitewashed houses are lying on the hills, they seem to be embracing the moonlight.

The outskirts of the villages have ample vegetation to a point of forming what seems like a tropical oasis in certain places with thick greenery of plants and trees. Around them are small garden farms which are surrounded by groves of trees, mainly olive trees.

The villages render images of other times, elements of times that regretfully we have given up. There exists a simple and a slower pace of life, elements that are close to the natural rhythms of nature.

The villages' square shaped houses are either white or brown. Most of those built with rough stones, have 'avli' (small courtyards) full of colourful pot plants in square whitewashed tins, which are often displayed in rows creating patterns like colourful parades spilling to the village streets. Many houses have pitched roofs that slope from one side to another. They also have outdoor woodburning ovens with faded white domes and blackened mouths where breads for each occasion are baked.

There is not one set style of house. Different elements blend together comprising different styles, but yet are simple and attractive. They compliment the landscape, not dominating it with a strong sense of art. The houses also blend in with the remaining Venetian structures.

Basically, the houses have a variable stonework around square, or oval shaped windows and arched doorways. The doors have a distinct feature: the door knobs with surrounding wood or metal plates are perforated and decorated with small designs. The type of houses vary according to the different locales and especially when they blend with the remaining Venetian buildings as manor houses. The remains are restored, for example, to utilize the space and to transform sheds and storerooms around cobbled courtyards extending the house, and for the rooms of the house to interconnect; for example, when you enter in one and exit in another, you can't help thinking, given the island's history, maybe that was another way for Cretans to elude their invaders in their searches.

Many villages are named after saints like the ones in the story, Aghie Apostoli, or Aghios Savas. Others included in the story like Anavolemata, Sternes, Demati, and Charaka are situated close to Messara plain, the richest plain in Crete.

Crete, with its picturesque villages, its contrasts of majestic mountain ranges, its abrupt landscape, gorges, contoured valleys, rivers and streams, surrounded by emerald blue water encircling ancient harbours, creates a picture of nature that will be imprinted on the visitor's mind for ever.

### Going to the Sea Under the Shadows

From the ancient site of Gortys, the descent to the Libyan Sea begins where the people in the story, under the shadows of the Germans, would traverse until they would see the water shining in the horizon of the Libyan Sea. The terrain opens into the vast valley of Messara where the villagers shielded and gave help to any partisans heading to meet the torpedo boat from the Middle East.

Many villages have formed around the rim of Messara as to allow a view to the valley plus to the surrounding mountains. The vista of Messara valley against the background mountains unfolds at the village Moulia. After passing a rugged landscape of rocks and big brown stones that comprise the mountain slopes, the road descends to the valley. In contrast, the terrain now grows patches of different greenery like wild flowers or grape vines and olive trees, until you get to Aghie Deka (meaning 'ten saints').

This town was named after ten bishops who were beheaded by the Romans for refusing to worship their gods. A small church marks the bishops' place of burial.

Lush greenery encircles the town, blending with Aghie Deka's traditional stone houses, making a picturesque background for paintings. Farther on and after passing a very small village of Ahgia Fotia the road leads to Mires, one of the towns with a wide view of the plain. Its quaint country houses are arrayed with masses of greenery on their porches, while grape vines hang from vertical and horizontal posts like cozy canopies.

Taking the road further west, you see the plain stretching to the horizon, when all of the sudden a row of eucalyptus trees appears on either side of the road. Passing under them, you feel like an honoured guest, welcomed by the whole valley. The trees end and after a little uphill climb you reach Characha, a village with much action: white houses, winding streets with scenes of Cretan life are all around. You could see older men riding horses, or leading mules, while women attend their little gardens.

Traveling further south and west amid greenery and olive trees, you will reach a serene white village, Sternes, after passing some huts where people gather to make the liquor 'raki' or 'tsikoudia'. When in season, you would see from afar sparks of fire on homemade ovens in the secluded, but to a degree, open huts.

Onward now, and you enter another village named Pyrgos, situated on the rim of the plain. It doesn't look to be on the edge of the land as you enter the village, but when exiting it is as if you're high on the mountains, a vast vista of the valley unfolds below you, with an imposing church in the middle of it. You're at such an angle that the church appears huge against the vast horizon as if dominating the valley and the background of the distant mountains.

Exiting the village and going into the valley you'll see the rich greenery of grape wines and olive trees of Messara framed by the Asterousia mountains which encircle the horizon. Going by the valley, you pass the village, Rotasi, a village with white rough country houses, sitting on a elevated rim of the plain. The view now is dominated by the mass of greenery of olive trees unfolding to the valley. As the road swings east you approach a big white and brown village, Mesochori. Traditional stone houses in brown and white blend with contemporary styled houses with framework windows and impressive staircases, and all built around a big church in the centre of the village.

A mountain range looms behind Mesochori. You would have the urge to be up there, at its peak, to enjoy the view of the plain. There is a road leading there which seems to lead you to the sky where you would think you'll be alone at the top of the world. You climb and climb the winding road entering another landscape no greenery, rugged wild mountain hills of brown scorched stones dominate the scenery up, but down is a whole panorama of Crete. As you climb thinking you reach the end of the world, there is some greenery, some green marks appear in the horizon. All of a sudden you enter a village, Achentrias. The authentic country atmosphere cannot fail to strike you. You would see scenes of country life you could only imagine today.

Stalwart figures of men in high boots ride on white handsome horses on the curved stone streets, with dogs hot in pursuit. Grand, rough, white stone houses with big wooden balconies loaded with firewood make a forceful presence. The houses with miniature gardens below, or a number of flower pots standing in attractive arrays are complimenting a picture of warmth and homeliness. But the setting is completed by stone framed windows in which intricate, handmade laced curtains hang, and through them peer curious faces, as they look at you, the visitor.

Then, the village's pathway leads you away to what seems to be the end of the road, or the mountain... but not in this space of the earth, not in this island of contrasts. The road leads you not where other mountains meet, but to a plateau, on the top of the world, that has green fields of plants sowed in elevation on one side creating a harmonious combination of green earth-colours, and rough mountains with wild vegetation on the other side, where animals graze peacefully. What a contrast! Cultivated greenery created by human mind and hand, on one side, and a wild natural wonder, on the other, but perfectly blending.

As the road bends, all of the sudden you realize you're not alone on the top of the world, but you're on a vista of mountain peaks. The way they rise into view make you think that they are rising in greeting, to acknowledge you, stretching as they do to the horizon, a relief map at your feet, the world is at your feet.

What a sensation of sight! A thrill of the senses, to feel an extension of yourself, of your very being, to be in harmony with nature, at one with the forces of the universe... you have the urge to challenge nature, to challenge yourself, to break the limits of yourself, to take risks... to be outrageous, to do the outrageous and the impossible... to jump from one peak to another singing - you control the world, it goes with your tune, every mountain and hill is as if offered on a silver platter from where you take your pick... as the circle of mountains ends and becomes one with the sea - to be one with the sensations of the sea.

Looking towards the horizon to the sea you can see Tsoutsouros, the final destination of the expeditions in the story, you can't help but to feel chills in your spine as you visualize how fifty years ago the Cretan people, under the shadows of the enemy, climbed to freedom, committed themselves to action for the sake of freedom, in doing their missions, while passing the pivotal points of their expeditions, the nearby villages of Achentrias, Sternes, Charaka, Demati, Metoxi, Fabriana, Vianno.

As the maze of these mountains surrounds those places, you won't help thinking that just the view of this land was enough to inspire and encourage the people to challenge themselves, to break their limits, as to be one with the beat of their land. Next you would think as the wind drops, to hear their voices...

"Ourah! at least I can go free," or "...that's the way it was... as it is in life at one time or another."

You might even have the illusion of seeing far in the horizon towards the sea, marks over the mountain peaks like a convoy '...a serpent of men, animals, and deadly weapons following behind...'

And then as the wind drops you think you hear "...no wonder these mountains with their abrupt changes of view and surroundings can influence you in having noble thoughts."

"Yes, indeed," you would say as if talking to yourself.

Then, going back on the road through an abrupt descent down to Messara plain around and more west, you reach the village of Kasteliana on the rim of the plain. Next, the village Metoxi appears pinned to a slope of the mountains. Going on further on mountain elevations and looking more towards the valley where rugged mountains dominate the horizon, you would see Basil's village, the village Favriana, which was a centre of underground activities during the war. Now Basil comes to take care of his land and to climb his beloved mountains.

As it is peace time, the village sits undisturbed on a mountain slope while the Messara plain with all its greenery is engulfing the mountains' feet. Quaint stone houses on different levels with the mountains in the background but in a closer range, the village offers a view to fit any painting. With the mountains appearing in deep green, brown, and copper tones from the shades of earth-colours, it is a contrast to the plain's lively green, but a harmonious one, a pleasant view to the eye. Next, after you pass Favriana you reach the village Demati. Entering the village, all of a sudden you are at the end of an abyss, a tremendous depth at your feet, a valley, a panorama of a green valley. Right at the edge you would see women knitting while enjoying the view. Seeing them you would feel the impulse to stop and look down, or wish to stay there to occupy yourself with some pastime. As you go on you would reach another village of the story, Skinia, a small traditional Cretan village sitting quietly on the plain, about four miles east of Favriana.

Due south of Basil's village is rough mountainous terrain ending at the rugged southern coast, Tsoutsouros, an area on the coastline loved by the bravest of fishermen and the hardiest of shepherds. It is wild, expansive and its tempestuous character was inhospitable to the Germans. In winter, it is inaccessible and in the summer Tsoutsouros may only be reached under certain conditions.

Coming back through the terrain and under the shadows of the ancient remains of Phaestos, following the scent of herbs, and climbing through clumps of wild sage, oregano and thyme spread in the fields, you reach the site of Aghia Triada. It is another Minoan site, where you can look down across the valley to the Libyan Sea, and feel a close connection to the sea. Under the shadows of ancient

Roman remains is the Minoan palace of Aghia Triada, a private palace with storage rooms, archival rooms and small sanctuaries as not to be exposed to the southern sun and be protected from the northern winds.

The southern coast is not far away, the road separates into two directions, either to Matala, a quaint village with an unusual, natural harbour and steep cliffs, or to Kali-Limenes where Saint Paul was shipwrecked. The cliffs sloping into the water have caves which appear like multiple mouths indented in a yellow grain of limestone rock. Those cliffs are like clumps of gigantic sponges ready to plunge into the sea, to absorb the foaming waves and to suck any unprepared swimmer into their caves... to forever vanish.

Then, closer to the sea in Rodisi, casting ancient shadows on the land there is a peaceful Byzantine monastery with pines surrounding its courtyard.

The road farther south and west to Phaestos can lead you to other summer places as Aghia Galini, a waterfront village sitting on a hill. White and blue houses, reflecting light from the sky and sea, are built on levels set on winding and curved paths that end in the sand. Warm silvery minuscule grains of sand spread over on the crispy beach, rising in the breeze, embrace and invigorate you with the salty cool spray of the sea... delicious.

Taking the road farther you wander by the Dikti mountain range viewing the rich countryside dotted with picturesque villages and small ancient churches, surrounded by subtropical vegetation. As you approach the village Avri, you will sense a change in atmosphere as you observe a dense grove of banana trees and groves of orange trees, golden shapes gleaming in the sun. Behind the fruit groves, is a gorge. Legend has it that an ancient god struck the rocky opening, which brought forth irrigating waters. When the wind blasts and it blends with the sound of the running water, a deafening thunder results, echoing for miles away.

From a pass viewing the Libyan Sea you arrive at Ano Viannos – a village perched high on the mountain slopes, surrounded by vineyards and olive trees. They surround the ancient church of Aghia Pelagia, with frescoes and icons from the fourteenth century. They also surround modern history as they are close to a monument to hundreds of Cretans executed for reprisals. When you exit the village the mountains' abruptness is at its best: a large abyss forming a gorge.

When you have experienced the environment of southern Crete, you can't help but be amazed how the people of the story managed to traverse the same routes; on their long treks, to the sea under the shadows of the enemy, they walked tremendous distances, stepping over rocks, over shrubs, crevasses, over hilltops, over abysses, and over sand in the dark, with the wind and rain beating at their faces, and with the sweltering heat licking their faces. During their expeditions, in conducting their operations, they had only the ghostly light of the moon, the shadows of the mountains, and the shadows of the ancient remains to guide them, with the sound of the water breaking on the beaches or the crying of the birds to accompany them.

# ΕΛΛΑΣ - GREECE

## Continuing the Journey

As you continue on your journey southeast you pass through rough countryside and coastline. Before approaching the southern seaport of Crete **Ierapetra** you come to **Amoudares**. In that area stand sand dunes with shapes that resemble the Pyramides.

Ierapetra faces the Libyan Sea and is one of the warmest areas of the island. Sunlight embraces the town almost all year round. Ieraptra's sandy seashore appears to be guarded by the remains of a Venetian castle which along with the Turkish minaret enhances the atmosphere. In this seaport town modern hotels and bungalows are set on terraced land along the coast. On some stretches of beach there are greenhouses from which their crops are shipped to the markets of western and northern Europe.

Leaving Ierapetra and moving along the rough coast for about twenty km. you reach the village of **Makri Yiallos**. Here there is one of the finest, and most secluded beaches at this eastern end of Crete. As the fine sand is being swept by the wind you can not help but start to think that a path may open for you to walk across... to Africa.

Moving northeast you reach the ancient sight of **Zakros** where there lies the remains of a Minoan town and palace near the coast; specifically it is at Kato Zakros, an eight km. hike down a rough road to the sea, which runs through an impressive gorge. Further north and passing through **Palecastro** you can see the contrast within a Cretan countryside: parcels of lush greenery and a barren landscape.

Past the palace site is the Valley of the Dead, a Minoan site of tombs. From Zakros you reach the village of **Palecastro**. Following the road you arrive at the Monastery of **Toplou** which stands in an isolated, almost intimidating place. The monastery has been a center of Cretan resistance against invaders. In the monastery is an eighteenth century icon depicting scenes from the Bible - a masterpiece.

From Toplou, you take the road leading northeast for some eight km. to find the beach of Vai. The road instead of revealing as you would expect either barren landscape or greenery, reveals a grove of exotic palm trees. You may wonder if you are in the Caribbean instead as you see a landscape stretching into the distance with palm trees and cliffs. Here you may find solitude if you wish. At this point we have completed our southern journey which began at Messara plain, where the partisans headed for their expeditions, to the farthest eastern part of Crete, Vai which is also close to the northern side of the island. From Vai and westward lies the whole northern part of Crete which is most densely populated, with its main seaport cities of Heraklion, Rethymnon, and Chania and the large but less populated towns of Aghios Nikolaos and Sitia.

Heraklion is a robust city, Rethymnon is more refined and Chania is a combination of both. **Heraklion**, the fifth largest city in Greece, is the governmental, administrative and commercial capital of Crete. Moreover, it has attractions of another era: Heraklion is the gateway to Knossos, the paramount Minoan site, and has a huge Venetian castle around its harbor.

Heraklion's power and vivacity has existed since ancient times, as indicated by its fortifications and the "Convent School of Mount Sinai", that has produced artists such as El Greko. Its massive Venetian circuit of walls were considered the strongest in the Mediterranean world during the fourteenth century. Sieging Turks took twenty-two years to penetrate the castle walls, in 1669. Heraklion's **Archeological Museum** thought by many to be one of the best in the world boasts a display of Minoan treasures.

**Rethymnon** has a unique, and intellectual character as it is the seat of a university. In the fourteenth century, Rethymnon produced the "Cretan Renaissance" with literary artists such as G. Hortajis with "Erofili" and Vincentos Cornaros with "Erotokritos", both epic works. Rethymnon maintains a harmonious blending of Venetian and Turkish elements which dominate the architecture of the city. The governing architectural element of the city is the large number of Turkish-style balconies -- curved, and often with railings -- protruding over the alleys, adding a mystical quality to the houses and mansions.

Although **Chania** has the legacy of an ancient city, it is more provincial and modern. In combination with its great sights the town is very stimulating to visit. An experience is when you approach the city and see the great White Mountains looming in the background, with their white snow-covered peaks on top of green hills.

Chania is encircled with a plain of citrus trees, and in season when the trees are full of blossoms, the scenery is filled with bright colors. Then there is the area of "Halepa" with its neoclassical-style houses and mansions which were built at the turn of this century. Beyond Halepa is **Acrotori**, a peninsula with a hill, on top of which lies the "tafos"(tomb) of Eleftherios Venizelos, a major Cretan political figure in modern Greek history. From there you can have a fine view of Rethymnon with ancient and modern architecture extending to the horizon.

In these three cities Heraklion, Rethymnon, and Chania, the old towns were built within Venetian walls and forts, such as the "Forteza" in Rethymnon, from where you can a have a panorama of the city. These castles have arches and arcades that stand as vestiges of past rulers: Venetians and Turks. The central squares -- the heart of these towns -- are traditionally planted with trees and shrubs, and are built around elaborate ancient lion fountains. It is here that the townsfolk gather for their "volta" (promenade), or sit at cozy outdoor cafes to engage in witty conversations with friends; one of their favorite subjects is "politika" (politics).

It is from these main northern cities of Heaklion, Rethymnon and Chania, that journeys can be taken to different parts of the island.

## Journeys from Heraklion

After visiting Knossos the road leading south turns to the small town of **Archanes**. The lush grape harvesting land of Archanes is a center of wine production. At one point on this road British and Cretan commandos abducted the German commander Kreiper. Archanes also has a Minoan site with a full view to the north.

From about twenty km. west of Heraklion the mountains take on every shade of brown and are marked with patches of greenery. At these mountains is the resort, **Aghia Pelagia**, with modern buildings set on elevated levels, and a beautiful sandy beach. Some twenty km. on, the road winds down behind some rugged mountains and reaches +Fodele+. The scenery here is made pleasant by fruit trees: orange, lemon and even olive trees grow on the surrounding hills.

At the center of Fodele is a stream crossed by a wooden bridge in a romantic setting amidst greenery, that sets the scene of a peaceful and contented Sunday promenade. It is also the village of the painter Domenikos Theotokopoulos, or El Greko as he was more commonly known.

Twenty km. southwest of Heraklion lies **Aghios Myron**. Outside the village is a large rock, which during bad weather emits white foam bubbles that scientists are still unable to explain. According to a legend it was a dragon that Saint Myron turned into a rock.

Twenty km. further south to the sea, there is the village of **Aghia Varvara** and then the village in our story **Gergeri** which has a fifteenth century Byzantine church.

Four km. further on, the road leads to the mountains to the big monastery of **Vrodisi**. The monastery's impressive entrance leads you to an inner courtyard which wafts with the scents of pines, palms, and orange trees. In the courtyard stands a fountain with engravings depicting Adam and Eve. The monastery holds masterpieces of paintings. Three km. after the next village **Voriza**, is the **Kamares** cave from where a climb to Psiloritis mountains can be started. Just a few km. further on from Aghia Varvara is the **Vourvoulitis** pass from where you have a wide view over the Messara plain.

If you take a journey east from Heraklion and along the coast you will see some of the most popular beaches on Crete.

At the distance of twenty-six km. there are **Amnisos** and **Mallia** that along with their natural beauty of sand beaches have the advantage of being almost city-like. In Mallia some modern buildings still have traditional outdoor ovens, and some flowered courtyards in front of business establishments.

After about fifty km. east, the road climbs into the mountains towards **Neapolis** -- a modern town with a provincial air. The scenery now reveals olive groves, sparkling water and rough land.

East from Neapolis you may see some old windmills close to the road spin their vanes as they catch the sprightly winds from the sea. Not too far to the windmills and after the villages of **Kasteli** and **Fourni** the landscape becomes rocky but has a raw, primitive beauty. From this vantage point you can see stretching onwards the Gulf of Mirabelo and the Sitia mountains.

## Journeys from Aghios Nikolaos

Above the Gulf of Mirabelo is the island's biggest holiday resort **Aghios Nikolaos**, which, some say, has a bottomless lake connected to the sea from an inner harbor. The lake and the harbor are surrounded by modern hotels, bungalows, pools and private beaches creating a "riviera" atmosphere. This cosmopolitan setting extends to Elouda, with its wild shrubs and a rocky sculptured beach, some ten km. due north. Luxurious bungalows and exotic out-door clubs have sprung up here.

Close to these modern places lies the most preserved Minoan town, Gournia, that sits between two low peaks. The site reveals , the remains of partly unearthed neighborhoods of the whole town. Stones, implements and tools, were found where they were originally used, which gives an impression of Minoan everyday life -- resembling in some ways contemporary civic life.

Onwards another twenty two km., and you come across **Pahia Ammos**, a fine beach in the narrowest section of Crete. From there the road goes south to the towns of Ierapetra, and north to Sitia. Another thirty five km. after Pahia Ammos and the villages of **Kavousi**, and **Mohlos** the road becomes one of the most dramatic in Crete, climbing steeply along the mountain cliffs, revealing tiers of orchards and olive trees.

Before Pahia Ammos, eleven km. from Aghios Nikolaos, there

lies the traditional village of **Kritsa**. The village clings to the steep mountainside and has a spectacular view over the Gulf of Mirabello. The village people even today maintain their traditional handicrafts and textile work. Every summer, there is a representation of a traditional wedding there. Before entering the village, in the middle of an olive grove sits a white church, the **Panagia Kera** (All Holy Lady). The frescoes on its walls from the fourteenth and fifteenth century display an overall originality and liveliness in Biblical scenes, were saints and evangelists are portrayed in rich gowns, muscular dimensions and with intense eyes. It was in Kritsa that the filming of the Kazantzakis novel "He who must die" took place. Before entering Kritsa a sign directs you to **Lato,** an ancient site from classical and Hellenistic times, with a beautiful view across the olive trees to the coast.

From Aghios Nikolaos the road goes south and then east, around the bay through some traditional villages such as in **Hamezi** where late in September there is a display of the makings of the Cretan popular drink "raki".

From there the road leads through the place of **Faneromeni** to the bay of the town of Sitia, to one of the biggest towns of Crete. Rugged mountains with patches of greenery are set in the background of Sitia. Its sandy beaches continue up to the palm-tree forest of Vai.

## Journeys from Rethymnon

Starting from Rethymnon, if you take the road southward you reach the intersection at Koxara after thirty km. or so. Nearby is the **Kourtouliotiko** gorge, named after the rattling sound made by pebbles and stones as they bump and roll down the river course. The whole atmosphere of stone clattering, of water splashing and of birds singing, is nature at its best. High up in the gorge ridges are five holes from which water springs, and, it is believed, that the holes are the imprints of Saint Nikolaos five fingers laid on the rock. Further on there is a little chapel at the end of a narrow path.

More south on the southern coast stands the **Monastery of**

**Preveli** which played a big role in Cretan resistance throughout history. The monastery displays many ecclesiastical items. The most notable one is a golden, miraculous cross which is said to contain a splinter of the cross of Jesus. One miracle is said to have happened during the German occupation of Crete. The Germans attempted to steal the miraculous cross. Three times they had tried to take the cross to Germany by aircraft, but each time the aircraft engines failed. Finally giving up, they returned the cross to its rightful place.

One km. away from the monastery there is a small river which leads down to an isolated beach. At this point where river meets sea, the area is profuse with palm-trees and tropical vegetation all the way to the seashore, to a sparkled sand beach washed by the Libyan Sea.

Further west along the coast from Preveli but higher in altitude is the village **Sellia.** Below it is the resort of **Plakias** which has new tourist developments and a wide stretch of beach with sand and scattered sculptured-like rocks. This beach, being close to gorges, has a beautiful blend of sand, stones, and sparkling water, that makes the countryside more serene, and offers serenity to the observer's hectic way of life.

Some thirty km. from Rethymnon on the way toward Matala is the cozy village of **Spili,** with shady trees and in the village square, bountiful water flows from nineteen ancient fountains with lion-like heads.

Travelling southeast toward the sea you pass the village and resort of **Aghia Galini**. A place not to miss if journeying from Rethymnon is the **Melidoni cave**, about fifty five km. east, and close to the town of **Perama**. The cave is worth visiting, not only for its natural attraction, but also for its history. It is full of stalactites and has a number of chambers. Acording to a legend the cave was the dwelling place of Talos, the mythical giant who wandered the island hurling stones at unwelcome visitors. Findings indicate that in ancient times, deities were worshipped in the cave. But one altar there is a reminder of more recent age. In 1824 several hundred Cretans died during a Turkish siege. The Turks trapped them inside, suffocating them by lighting a fire at the cave entrance.

After the Melidoni cave the road turns south for about six km. to the village of **Margarites**. The villagers to this day maintain their centuries old tradition of hand-making pottery and ceramics, as the making of the large "pithoi" Minoan pots.

Travelling towards Rethymnon you can go to Chania; the westward leading road to Chania makes a zig-zag, climbs the mountains, then descends to the coast passing Crete's only lake, **Kournos**. The lake, reflecting the contrasts of the surrounding countryside, sometimes appears to change colors. This road also bypasses areas of quiet beaches, the bay of Souda and the place of "Kokino Horio" where the filming of "Zorba the Greek" took place.

Inland and towards the mountain Psiloriti, at about fifty-three km. southeast from Rethymnon, is a village in our story, **Anogia,** from which you can reach the center of the island into the Ida plateau. At the edge of the plateau in a rugged, wild landscape lies the Ida cave. Bronze shields, gold jewellery and many other objects were found with an altar in that cave. It is here where you will find traces of the traditional mountain life of Crete, such as being able to see shepherds who live in stone houses called "mitata" just as they have done for hundreds of years.

About thirty-five kilometers from Rethymnon, you should not miss the lush valley of **Amari.** A short trip southeast from Rethymnon will bring you to the **Monastery of Arkadi**, that played a major role in the island's history. The monastery with its facade being one of the most ornate Venetian structures in Crete is a refined contrast to the surrounding wild landscape. The monastery had been the center of underground activities during the island's Turkish occupation. It was in November 1866 that the Greeks who were sieged in the monastery by an overwhelming number of Turks, chose to die, by bombing themselves, rather than capitulate. The monastery still shows traces of the bloody fighting. Their attitude -- freedom or death -- is commemorated every year on the eighth of November.

## Journeys from Chania

Just six kilometers north of Chania by the base of Souda is the **Acrotiri peninsula,** with a beautiful view and the big **Monastery of Aghia Triada**. All along the coast near Chania, dramatic World War II battles took place. One such battle took place at **Maleme**, nineteen km. west of Chania. Twenty-three kilometers from Chania is **Kolimbari**, a quiet place with a sheltered beach; then, the road leads into the peninsula of **Rodopou** where the **Monastery of Gonias** is. It offers a beautiful view that gives a serene image to the monastery. But more unique are a number of Turkish cannon balls lodged in its walls.

Going west, about forty-two kilometers, at the end of the main road in a region full of vineyards and olive trees is **Kastelli**, a town with a rocky beach and a harbor. Further south in contrast to the west of Kastelli the beaches are more refined as are the beaches by the villages of **Falassarna** and **Kabos.** Beyond both is the monastery of **Chrysoskalitsa**, meaning the Golden Step. The convent is so named because of ninety steps leading to it. The steps are said to be made from gold which can only be seen by a pure, sinless person.

Before reaching the monastery, however, you will pass villages among chestnut groves. In one, **Elos**, a festival is held every October with traditional music, and a specialty is served, chestnut cakes: a welcoming sight for visitors. Following the road through **Platanias** and Elos provides a stunning scenery. You'll see the contrast of the Cretan countryside at its best: villages clinging to the hillsides among olive trees and chestnuts, and the sea glittering below. South of Elos the road becomes rougher as it leads to high rough mountains. After the mountainous ride you would welcome the changing of scenery, that is the coastal town of **Paleohora**. But before getting in Paleohora, a road some fifty-three km. from Chania will lead you to **Kandamos** with its profuse greenery. Kandamos was completely burned by the Germans during the World War II. Today there is a sign still reading: "Kandamos once existed." You get the impression when visiting this region that you are in a kind of “Wild West”: the area is rough with gorges, high mountains and steadfast inhabitants.

The Omalos plane is about thirty-nine kilometers from Chania and is the last stop before the hike to **Samarian Gorge.** To the far end of the gorge is the village of **Aghia Roumeli** whose inhabitants are involved with traditional occupations such as cattle-breeding and herb gathering.

From Aghia Roumeli is **Hora Sphakion** the capital of Sphakia region. From Hora Sphakion some twelve km. to the east is **Frangokastello**, a fortress that the Venetians built in the fourteenth century. As the castle lies by the sea, it gives an air of mystery to the coast. Ghosts were seen, it is claimed, of hundreds of Sphakians who died defending their fort against the Turks in 1828. In early May, at dawn these soldiers, “drossoulites”(dawn shades) appear on the castle walls. Scientists explain this phenomenon as a mirage from Libya.

At the southermost point of Crete and of Europe is the small wild island of **Gavdos**. It is about thirty-seven km away, from Crete. The island is full of history. There is a cave where the nymph **Calypso**, the one who detained **Odysseus**, is supposed to have lived. During Turkish rule the island was a refuge, and during World War II fighting took place there between German and British forces.

The Monastery of Preveli at the southern coast of Crete.

A seaside.

Sunset in Arvi

Elounda bay

The beach of Vai.

Cretans in local uniform.

Cretan dance.

The entrance of the palace in Phaestos.

An entrance passage to the palace of Knossos.

The Queen's Megaron in Knossos.

View of Messara Valley.

The plateau of Lasythi.

A picturesque village.

*Photographs are courtesy of Drossos Bross Publishing House Heraklion.*

# SECTION TWO

# BASIL'S STORY

**To love one's country,**
**to love one's environment...**
**To the younger generations.**

**Basil**

## LIFE AT THE BEGINNING OF THE WAR

We were a large family, and, in truth, we worked like slaves to support ourselves. My father was a shepherd. My parents were from the village of Anogia on the island of Crete. They had bought only a few household things when they first married; then they had eight children.

The first child was a top student and they sent him to medical school. At that time a good education was hard to get and the parents who had children in universities or colleges sacrificed everything for them. In 1931, when my father died, we were in debt, but by the time the war came we had made some progress, and everything was going smoothly. My eldest brother Costas, became a doctor. After him were two more sons, (the third was myself), followed by my three sisters, Chrysi, Maria, Ariadni, and finally there were the babies of the family a boy and a girl, Michalis and Vagelio.

As we lived in villages, it was easier for us to get acquainted with each other and to cultivate intimate relationships. Marriages, baptisms and religious celebrations were our opportunities for family ties to be strengthen and to unite us in understanding and respecting each other.

These bonds were reinforced by the need to reach for others to overcome the hardships of the following turbulent pre-war times. The bonds of sharing and helping one another created the base and support to toil over our land and to withstand the hard conditions before the war, the political changes, the global economic depression, bad harvests, famine, sickness, and even death.

We felt inseparable from our land because throughout history we have thrown off many oppressors, one more conqueror couldn't make a difference. That's the way it was before the Second World War; nevertheless, we had worked hard like slaves to get out of debt, to recoup our losses and for the eldest to be educated.

At that point the war caught up with us. We fell under the dictatorship of Metaxa, but even though we were anti-government nothing happened to us. In 1940, the Italians moved aggressively against Greece. As a result of that, a desire to defend our land grew.

I found myself in the army, with military insignia on my uniform and ready to fight for my country.

On October 28th, 1940, when war was declared, I was with the Greek army in Trikala moving towards northern Greece. From there our artillery marched at full speed for four days until we arrived at the place called Kalpaki, on the border of Greece. The Italians were already there. There the Greek army fought, how can I say it? with such confidence, with such enthusiasm.... I cannot put it in words. We attacked the Italian positions and we made the Italians run for their lives. Then we moved on to a place called Tepeleni where we again fought them successfully.

Since the Italians could not defeat us, the Germans launched an attack and broke our northern strongholds. We had to retreat. In a place named Klesoura, we made our last stand and used our last artillery. Then, we were pushed back to Kalpaki where we had fought with pride against the Italians. This time we were forced to surrender to the Germans and leave all cannons. We were forced to retreat, heading south. Eventually I had to cross the Athens waterfront, Pireas, where I was supposed to get on a boat to go to my island.

This journey was not a tranquil ride through pleasant countryside. Escaping south through the roads was like navigating a turbulent river - through a rugged terrain, potholes and craters caused by German bombardment that swirled us and steered us off course. Our little vehicle - an old car which someone had found - was tossed this way and that way swaying violently. I will never forget that the car with its wheels spinning, spraying us with mud, loaded up with people hanging out from doors and windows, tilted dangerously, like a dinghy in rough seas. The weather fought us, heaven cried over us... The mountains hid their faces in the clouds; or maybe the ancient Gods hid their faces from what was happening to us and the rain that soaked us was their judgement.

Small houses, broken and squalid with patches of gardens, passed by us as we were carried forward in that little car, towards the sea way south.

Suddenly, we came out on a peaceful valley laying before us. Untouched by the disaster of north Greece, the golden light played over Thebes as it had for thousands of years.

We continued on to arrive at the Athens waterfront, the port of Pireas, the end of the land that strung at the water barrier in front of us, glittered blue, beyond which were unattainable islands, the farthest of them, mine.

It struck me that we were now refugees.

It is my opinion that in the battle of Crete which had just taken place, two mistakes had been made. Firstly, those in command should have withdrawn the Cretan division from the borders sooner and sent it to defend Crete. Secondly, the government should not have taken the weapons away from the Cretan military bases. The government had issued an order that the army was to have all available armaments to defend the Greek borders.

While I was north, Crete was unarmed and unmanned, missing its strength and lifeblood to fight the battle of Crete. Those that should have fought the Germans were wandering around, mixing with the hurrying confused crowd. I became just one more desperate face among the innumerable distressed who filled the city, one more devoid of hope, devoid of livelihood.

I desperately sought a way back to my island. Every day, I would go to the harbor, and the city, spending my time in cafes and public places, anywhere looking for acquaintances and connections. I sought for anyone who could help me get back to Crete.

As I said, if they hadn't taken the weapons from Crete the outcome of the battle might have been completely different. Whatever losses Hitler suffered there, he suffered at the hands of native men and women who had only rudimentary makeshift weapons.

Day after day, night after night passed as I desperately searched to find a way back home. Only home could sustain me and cushion me giving me the strength to cope with the blows of war. That was my dream.

I tried and tried and sometimes it seemed there was no way to achieve my goal, only bleakness and hopelessness and people dying from hunger in the streets. But deep down I was confident that when I returned home I would be afraid of neither the Germans nor of hunger. I'm sure others felt the same way. It was one of the most agonizing times of my life.

One day, I met somebody who was a captain of a caique, a small fishing boat. He agreed to take some of us to Paros, an island in the direction of Crete. The Italians were in command on Paros but even so the situation there was more relaxed because the Italians were less strict than the Germans. How can I characterize the

Italians? They were easy-going.

I, along with some compatriots, set off to Paros. As we approached the island it seemed to be untouched by war. Its colours hit my eyes. The island was brilliant white, set like a diamond between sapphires of sky and sea.

Upon arrival, the people welcomed us and took care of us as much as they could. They took us to their houses which were dotted over the hillsides, painted in Greek island colours: whitewashed walls, with windows and door frames painted in bright blue, together complimented nature's surroundings. It was another world, full of hopes and expectations. That's how it was!

We all felt like brothers with each other. The captain went to the Italians and got a permit to carry cargo to Crete and we were free to sail again. We had left Athens secretly, but this time we left the Italian headquarters at Paros with a permit, and sailed off freely at dawn for Crete.

All we wanted was to set foot on our beloved land, a region of rugged mountains, of caves, of gorges and deep golden plains, all encircled by blue and emerald waters. I remembered the pre-war years, toiling over the sweet soil, tending my farm and my animals. Here was my land, my livelihood. We arrived in Crete as the sun was setting and I gazed on the outline of my beloved land, dimly reflected in the darkening waters.

The minute we approached the port, a German patrol boat came alongside. They didn't want us to dock. Soldiers came on board and said: "Whoever moves is going to die on the spot."

The local people had learned of our arrival and city officials came to the boat and described conditions on Crete. They said to us, "Here it's like the dead crying for the living while the living are crying for the dead. What do you want here?"

All we wanted was to go home again to the villages we knew. After the discussions and arguments, the Germans decided to deport us that same night. Our captain was very smart and he tried to make any number of excuses, like the need to repair the caique, and that he was out of diesel. We tried everything; we showed them the permit again and again, but they were adamant.

"Take them to wherever you brought them from," they told our captain, and we left.

Even before we sailed out of the harbour, we had decided not to go back to Paros. The captain was very sympathetic to our feelings.

He understood when we told him, "We know that wherever we're going, we risk death. Any other island will be just as dangerous place for us as Crete."

The captain agreed to take us wherever we wanted to go and we were united in our choice. We wanted to land somewhere else in Crete. He set sail towards the Greek mainland until late that night, and in the darkest hours he turned silently back towards Crete. We passed a place named Dia, and then we changed course and headed for Sises. In the darkness, the captain struggled to maneuver the boat for us to land.

Eventually we were then able to get ashore. Standing on Cretan soil at last I bent down, picked up some soil and kissed it. In the deep darkness and alert for the slightest sound, we gathered in one spot. Then we noticed a light and two or three of us went towards the light only to discover that it came from an old mill. We needed to find out if there were any Germans nearby. The rest of us waited for the all-clear signal.

At the mill we met some local people, and when we told them who we were, they greeted us with enthusiasm and cheered. One of them left and notified the village, and after a while others came to see if they could help in any way. They showed us good hospitality and we stayed there until morning.

In the morning we split into groups and discussed where to go because we came from different places like Chania or Lasithi. There were about seventy of us all together. I wanted to avoid the areas that were already occupied by the Germans, but others said that they would go to the capital city of Heraklion which had been taken over.

I said, "I'm not going to set a foot in any German occupied territory."

I left and I went to my parents' village Anogia, a rugged village away from the city, where the Germans had not yet come. At this time their army was stationed in only a few cities of Crete.

On the twenty-seventh of July, 1941, I arrived in Anogia. My mother saw me. Until that time, she hadn't known if I was dead or alive. All my friends and relatives were happy to see me. They hugged me and questioned me about my war experiences. It was as if they were trying to recapture the part of my past that they had missed.

In Anogia I learned that some Englishmen were staying in my winter cabin up in the mountains. They were part of the allied forces that had fought in the battle of Crete. There were Englishmen,

New Zealanders, Australians, and Cypriots. After the retreat, these soldiers were forced south, to the area of Tsoutsouro, which was a deserted point near the coast. They lived in the caves under primitive conditions waiting and watching in desperation for allied ships to appear on the horizon and rescue them. While waiting they needed to find a safe place to stay where there were no Germans until they could leave. In the meantime I, along with other villagers, went to Tsoutsouro to take them food. It was here that I had my first meeting with the organizers of the resistance, and I decided to join the forces that they were forming.

The most important thing the resistance forces had to accomplish at that time was to support and to find food for the allied soldiers who were in hiding. Although it was hard because food supplies were running out, with the willing help of the local populace we gathered food any way we could.

We also tried to encourage the local people and raise their morale that was at a low ebb after the battle of Crete. The people were panic stricken as the Germans were very vindictive. I knew for example, that the Germans even made people dig their own graves before they shot them. The whole island suffered.

Because I had many family and social connections in the villages, I was put in charge of gathering food for the refugees. To do this, I and others went from house to house and village to village gathering food for them.

People would give us all the food that they could spare like meat, bread, cheese, and olives. We would take it to the caves where the fugitives lived and then they would cook it and distribute it among themselves.

In these early days of the German occupation, we could move freely between the villages. Gradually, hatred of the Germans grew and the resistance movement took shape, helped by such people as Raftoupoulos, Koumentakis, Souris, Fakaros, and others.

One day, a Captain Stefanos Delivasidis, along with some English men and some Greeks, decided to rebuild an old fishing boat. They found oars and everything they needed for that. When it was finished, it was christened Argo. On the sixteenth of September, 1941 the boat left on its first mission, carrying ten or twelve persons heading for the Middle East and Egypt. When they arrived they explained to the people in command of the allied forces that there were still some unoccupied areas in Crete and that there was a resistance movement. They suggested that a radio transmitter could be set up.

One night while sitting in front of a makeshift house by the harbor, in Tsoutsouro, we saw a glint of light in the sea. We didn't pay any attention at first, but we saw a second and a third gleam. One of us, an experienced sea captain in the first World War suddenly cried out, "A submarine! A submarine! That's a submarine! Make a fire!"

Right away we started signal fires. We signalled that all was clear and an English officer disembarked. He came ashore followed by two other men who carried a radio transmitter. Whatever the visitors had to say was said only to the local commanders.

At that time I was just a news carrier, an ordinary guy who was running errands. In the following weeks and months other submarines came and once even a torpedo boat. Unfortunately there was no organization among the various resistance forces and nothing was accomplished. This situation continued until the January of 1942.

On the first of January our weapons came in a torpedo boat. We stored them in a cave that was used by guerilla groups of Captain Petrakogiorgis and Captain Badouvas. As I said before, the southern part of Crete wasn't occupied at this time. The Germans had passed through as if they were taking a walk, but they hadn't seen anything to interest them, they hadn't discovered anything.

One night Captain Badouvoyiannis came to get weapons, but he had a disagreement with one of the English officers who was helping our resistance group. The English officer said that he needed Souris, the translator, to be present when the twelve arms were handed over to Captain Badouvoyiannis.

During the argument, a message arrived saying that some 1,500 Germans were coming towards us. We were in grave danger, our meeting place was confined with no room to escape; furthermore, the bare winter ground clearly showed our footprints, and the broken branches and twigs would have given the Germans a clue that people had met here.

I left with Captain Badouvoyiannis to hide the weapons. The English officer reluctantly gave them to us. We figured that we had to save the weapons no matter what so that the Germans wouldn't find them and take revenge on the people; moreover, we thought it would be demeaning for us if the Germans seized the first shipment of arms to the resistance movement.

We sent a message to the villages and people arrived early in the morning with animals to carry the weapons for us. It was decided to hide the armaments in my winter place, in Harakia, which was close to the sea, about half to three-quarters of an hour from the village.

The Germans never came; the message had been wrong. I never found out why; however, the Germans did arrive a few days later. They didn't find anything, but they took a villager, named Michael, and his wife with them. It seems that he later betrayed our activities to the Germans. Although he was from Heraklion, he had lived in Tsoutsouro for quite a while and he had known what was going on there.

A few days later the Germans surrounded the area. They were looking for George Goumentakis, who like me was one of the first freedom fighters - he had been betrayed by Michael. Fortunately Goumentakis was able to escape by leaving through the back door of a house.

He had been notified in time by a code we used when warning others of approaching Germans. It went: "Rams, rams... The rams are coming," (the rams were the Germans).

In the scramble to escape ten people were captured: John, George and Charalampos Papadakis, John Kefalakis, Vlamis Plichronis, Charalambos, and Nick Petrakis. As far as I know, the Germans killed these people. Until then, our part of the island had not been occupied. It was as if the Germans didn't exist, but from that time, the Germans burned the Tsoutsouro area and put outposts on the southern shores.

The whole of southern Crete including the area of Tsoutsouro and a fifteen kilometre area around the Asterousia range of mountains was declared a dead zone. Anything that moved was to be shot on sight, German outposts were everywhere, even the goats, which had grazed on these lands, were driven out. It was a struggle to survive and as time went by things became worse.

It was difficult for our people to remain united in the face of adversity. We, the members of the resistance, went from village to village, talking to the villagers. We said to them: "We are Greeks and we should follow our ancestors' examples. We should not let the Germans occupy Crete and do nothing, as if we don't care".

With such talk, and with patriotic songs, wherever and whenever we could, we tried to fire their spirit of patriotism and raise their morale, so that they would help in the fight against the enemy. I traveled with my friend Captains Petrakogeorgis, Podias and Samaris.

The resistance to the German occupation now covered the whole of Crete; we were united with no political overtones to the movement at this time. It was a vital time and the Greeks had to show what it meant to be Greek. The Germans weren't able to find out anything about what was going on because all the local people – about ninety-five per cent of them – were working with us. Part of eastern Crete, a whole district, held out until the last remaining fugitives from the battle of Crete had left on allied ships. In other words, a real Judas didn't exist among us. On the whole, we were all united for our cause in cooperating with each other, and everybody knew my hiding place, even women and children. There was only one instance of betrayal.

One time the Germans were looking for me because somebody had betrayed me. I think the person who informed on me did it out of fear. The person I suspect, I don't want to say his name, was a co-fighter whom I had recruited into our resistance forces. On one mission the Germans caught him, after which he was tortured until he gave them our names. Then the Germans killed him. From then on there weren't any other instances of betrayal from our people.

### The Goats

Before I left for Amari, I had my first close encounter with Germans because of some goats. One day I saw several of them shooting at some goats which were scattered in a field. The Germans were using them as target practice, I suppose, or just passing time, but as they were at a distance, although they tried and tried, they didn't hit any.

I was afraid they might kill or injure someone or something other than a goat, so I went over and said that if they would let me use a gun, I would show them how to shoot. They did, and I hit a goat and killed it. The Germans enthusiastically said to me, "Good, good, you're good," and laughed.

That was the first time I was close to any Germans, and I thought, well... maybe some Germans are different.

Probably that's what I had in mind in another similar incident involving animals, also at the beginning of the German occupation.

At the beginning of the occupation, as I said, the Germans had proclaimed the area Tsoutsouro a dead zone, although animals were left to wander in those fields. Since they were used to being there, the animals would stray and go there again and the Germans would kill them for food.

The resistance wasn't in full force yet, so I didn't fear the Germans and probably we were not yet used to them being here. Thus, one day I had the nerve to take my younger brother, who knew a little of the German language, to go to a German guard station to find out what had happened to my animals that had been grazing around that area.

Young and fresh we arrived there. Outside the station, laying lazily and relaxed, enjoying the sunshine, were some shirtless Germans.

"Sun... good," I said with a smile, pointing to the sun.

"Yeah! Yeah!" they replied easily, grinning.

Then, my brother, who was behind me, lurched in front of me with a let's get to the point attitude, and he said pointing at them: "What... happened to... animals?"

"Nein, nein," they said.

"Animals... here..." my brother insisted seriously, as if inspecting them.

"Nein, nein," the Germans kept saying, as they began to rise, looking at us angrily.

Then farther, we noticed a big pot over the fire emitting steam. "There... are our animals," my brother said..."proof... proof..."

He pointed to the pot, at which point the Germans turned their heads towards to the pot, then towards us, showing surprise.

With a sudden impulse I ran to the pot with my hands waving in the air. "There... I got you. I have the proof."

I went closer and closer to the pot and lifted the lid.

"Here is my meat... your dinner at my own expense." I murmured again and again as I lifted the lid. I looked into the pot and I was blinded by the steam. I couldn't make out if there was meat cooking or anything in the pot at all. Where is the elusive meat? Where is it? I thought, as I bent more, looking but seeing no meat in sight.

I tried to find another explanation as I looked into the German's eyes which, by now, were growing bigger and bigger with consternation. Perhaps, I thought, I would have to face the possibility that there was no meat at all in the pot, only water, but why only water?

I looked at the Germans, and paid more attention to the fact that none of them were wearing shirts, then the answer came to me; they were boiling water to do their laundry!

And that's how it was.

The Germans lurched towards us, their eyes in agitation, their bodies in mobilization, their hands in apprehension while we started running in the opposite direction shouting in desperation.

"Okay, okay. Nein, you... didn't... our animals..."

And the Germans shouting back "Go to hell!"

## The Lost German

One day, I was high on a mountain slope, sitting on a big rock, relaxed and undisturbed, watching my animals grazing in the nearby fields. It was a picture of total peace, only nature surrounded me with its brilliant sky and the rusty, golden brown colours of the earth. It was a vision of harmony. Everything was calm and serene to a point of stillness.

All of a sudden, a shadow fell across me. I turned around and heard a voice say in German, "See... see... soldier."

The shadow deepened as soldiers appeared from behind me. I glanced back and I distinguished a military figure with broad shoulders and big hands waiving some papers. Then, a stern mouth saying, "See... see... soldier..."

He was a German commander of the area, and behind him were four or five other soldiers.

"See... soldier..." the commander kept saying.

I looked around at the hillside and I saw a young German soldier climbing unsteadily, stumbling to find his way between the mountain crevices and gullies. I pointed out the soldier to the commander. The commander called him but the soldier, stumbling over rocks near the crevices, had difficulty coming down. He couldn't find a good path, trying to find his way out of the mess he was in. I suggested to my shepherd, who had now appeared, that he should go where the German soldier was, to help him find his way.

The officer was pleased. He grinned at me as he pulled out cigarettes and he offered me one. We smoked in silence watching the progress of the rescue. He indicated the papers in his hands, and I shrugged.

"I don't read any German," I said, half in German half in Greek. "Nein diavaso German."

"I teach," he replied, and pointed to the first word.

I tried to pronounce it and he laughed. I laughed too.

The shepherd by this time had reached the soldier and they were returning. We were happily puffing away at our cigarettes when other Germans must have come into the area because a call rang out and echoed through the hills, "Rams, rams... the rams are coming."

The shepherds giving the warning couldn't see me, but they knew I was in the area; however, they had not seen the Germans I was talking to.

I waved my arms wildly trying to make the shepherds stop shouting. The officer looked at me. I tried to make it look as if I was clearing smoke from my eyes, and I pointed to the cigarette. The officer didn't smile.

The call came again. I waved again. The soldiers with the commander were in full alert now. The shepherds kept calling and the other patrol came even closer. I began to cough and splutter as if chocking in the cigarette. The commander looked all the way to the hillside, his blue eyes coldly suspicious.

'I need the hand of one of the gods, like in tragedy', I thought.

"Here he is," a voice rang out, as my shepherd and the young German waving his arms, came into the view.

"Here he is," I called again in Greek, so the whole hillside could hear.

'The signal is going to get me killed', I thought fearfully.

Everything stopped. The last echo of the warning faded away, raams…aams.

I coughed.

This time I coughed really, loudly.

The Germans dropped their weapons and the commander thumped me on my back.

"You okay?" he said.

"Yes, Yes," I said spluttering.

He collected his papers together and brought his soldiers to attention.

"Danke schone, thank you," he said, and they left.

You may be wondering about the other patrol. They appeared too, but kept their distance from the 'big commander' as they called him because they were, the ones we called 'German beggars', who went to the villages, asking for food and things.

And is that the end? No!

I learned afterwards that the commander had been to my village and the papers he wanted to teach me to read were for my arrest! He had been looking for me. It was the time that I had been betrayed and they had come to arrest me.

When the Germans came to my house, my mother behaved very cleverly. She told them that I wasn't her real son, that I was her step-son, and that I didn't consider her as my mother because we didn't have any contact over the years. The translator was good and it worked.

In any case, I stayed in the mountains where I could not get caught. When I needed to, I would go to my village in the daytime, carefully, like a bird that flies low inspecting the ground.

## THE ROLE OF THE RESISTANCE IN CRETE

The Germans killed many people and destroyed much property in retaliation for the strong resistance the Cretans put up against them in what came to be known as the Battle of Crete.

Most of that time I was in Athens, trying to find a way to get back home. The Germans proclaimed that all opposition would be dealt with severely. And they carried out their promises of punishment. In some cases the locals, or allies, would cut telephone wires, or commit other acts of sabotage. In retaliation, the Germans either would take the local people as prisoners for compulsory work in the German bases or they would demand that the people living in the surrounding villages bring, for example, five thousand of kilos of oil by a certain time. If the villagers were not able to fulfill the order, some would be taken and imprisoned or be executed.

Also the Germans declared that for every one of their soldiers killed, a hundred Greeks would be executed. With conditions like that we, the resistance forces, had to be careful not to give the Germans any reason to harm people. We only did whatever the allied headquarters instructed us to do, like cooperating with the sabotage of the enemy's airbases and installations, or sabotage actions in progress by the Germans that in a way it wouldn't look that they were done by local resistance forces. All direct clashes with the Germans was avoided.

When the Germans came to get food, such as cheese, milk or meat, the locals could easily have trapped them and killed them, but in truth, nothing would have been accomplished, for the Germans would have burned whole villages in reprisals. It was different for the people to continue their passive resistance when they knew that was a force in the mountains to protect them, and to offer refuge to them when was the danger of the Germans prosecuting them.

We had to instruct people on how to avoid confrontations and what to do when they encountered difficult situations. When we rebels were in villages gathering food, information, or guiding people, we were never sure what we would encounter so we carried small weapons that could be easily hidden.

We had to be especially careful when we encountered German patrols. I remember one incident in the village of Aghie Apostoli. We had gone there to collect food and to talk to the villagers who were gathered in the church. As I left, the priest wanted to talk to me and he escorted me part of the way. Shortly we saw six Germans on horseback only one hundred meters away. When the priest saw them, he was afraid and said to me, "Run away!"

My gun was hidden underneath my coat and because of that, the priest was afraid, for if the Germans searched us, it would have meant certain death for both of us. The area was flat and open, and I could not run away without looking suspicious. I told him that I wouldn't run, that it was not a wise move and for him to act normaly. When he saw that I was not willing to go, he left me and went towards some pasture where animals were grazing, so it would seem, if the Germans caught me, that he didn't have anything to do with me. I continued acting casually and the Germans just passed by without paying any attention.

Incidents like this happened lots of times. Whenever we faced Germans unexpectedly, or met patrols, had we let our fear show, it could have easily lead to a skirmish, and that's what we were trying to avoid. We were in the position to meet their superior war machine face to face, by trapping unsuspecting Germans or making the sabotages more catastrophic; however, we chose to sneak up from behind, inflict damage, and then vanish leaving them bewildered. We didn't want to give the Germans any reason to retaliate against particular villagers or innocent people and lead to ruin of whole areas.

The purpose of German reprisals was not just to punish, but also to demoralize the people and discourage them from giving assistance to the resistance. That's why the resistance fighters were careful; we didn't want to be the cause of misery to the people who showed us so much love and consideration as they helped us.

The Cretans gained great moral support with the knowledge that there was a force in the mountains to protect them and offer refuge to them in times of danger when they continued their passive resistance.

Because of this the people formed a network with us against the enemy. As the Germans took over the island and set their military installations with all their technical means and the advantages of the conqueror, we Cretans had only our 'human wireless stations' to depend on. It was a human chain that linked the villages, the mountains and the valleys, transmitting by word of mouth the enemy's movements.

All the allies' planned actions in sabotage or planned air attacks would have been detected by the Germans as they had radar aerials, and instruments such as radio detection and radio receivers to pick up ally communication lines. Only when there wasn't enough time the resistance would take the risk of using their own transmitter pertaining the upcoming bombardments. Besides reporting German movements, the messages sent by our human chain were to prepare for the arrival of our saboteurs and their explosives, instruments or equipment.

As the Germans were alien to our island, we had to counter them with only our knowledge of our environment. In knowing every inch of our soil, every rock and every tree, we were able to defend it. We banded together and fought a continuous battle against the enemy with our passive resistance.

The people had formed an invisible network of command. They had divided the area into regions of operations where certain individuals would take charge giving responsibilities to others lower in command. One method of collecting information was to send out scouts to explore areas and follow German movements.

The information the people were looking for concerned the direction of different German patrols inspecting the areas, how many Germans worked in administrative offices, what buildings were occupied by them, how many Germans were in each section at any given moment, what were their armaments, what were their routine routes. Furthermore, with the cooperation of the people who were doing compulsory work in the German buildings, or air fields, we could learn who were the commanding officers and their functions on each particular installation.

Information was passed on by messengers from one area to another to various resistance groups located at different bases at the Cretan countryside. In turn, for fast contact these resistance fighters would communicate using the radio transmitter, with our allies in the Middle East. Based on this information, the allied forces would send commandos from the Middle East to sabotage the enemy's bases and installations.

My village, Favriana, was located in a hill about a kilometre from the mountains. It was the centre of coordination and communication between the different local resistance groups, British intelligence and the Americans.

The couriers and representatives from other resistance groups, or the English, who had to get in contact with us, didn't go directly to our headquarters, but first had to be screened. This process was set up for security reasons to avoid infiltration by German agents.

A day didn't pass without visitors coming to my village. If, for any reason, any of these people acted suspiciously, then they would be detained, or killed if necessary.

Our most important mission was to support and assist the clandestine sabotage units that came to Crete from the Middle East. We had to be in contact with the allies - dangerous enough if the Germans found the transmitter - but we also met the torpedo boat bringing arms and ammunition, for defense, or explosives such as time bombs, for sabotage missions.

In these particular operations other local people, our guides, would play an important role. They not only acted as couriers, but also and most importantly, led different resistance groups or ally units to various destinations, traversing great distances, to hit the enemy's bases or prepare and plan sabotage. The guides had an uncanny knowledge of pathways and trails in Crete's steep mountains and rugged valleys, that the Germans never knew existed. The best guides would save time and lives by taking us though safe pathways that even locals did not know. They would also take charge of the animals that constituted convoys for our missions for the Middle East.

In the dark, on expeditions, the guides not only had to lead us to our destinations, but also had to manage those 'undercover' animals, so as not to make a sound at the wrong time or the wrong places.

On expeditions, under the shadows of the Germans, local people would hide the commandos in their houses and give them shelter, food or clothes to wear if necessary so that they would look more like we Cretans. They also gave supplies, like food or water, to take until the next stop. Local people would even help the commandos carry their arms and ammunition when they had great distances to go. And all this while the danger was that the wrong eyes would see them (there existed a real small minority of German sympathizers and agents) as had happen, for many Cretans were executed for assisting the resistance. It is amazing to know what impossible lengths these ordinary people were prepared to go through to help the resistance and when caught refused to divulge what they knew, as it is demonstrated in the story of our guide Manolio.

During the day, we in the resistance forces moved freely from place to place. It was easy for the local people to warn us of danger in daytime, but at night, because of German curfews and darkness it was impossible and dangerous. During the day, before setting off from our base in the mountains, we would be notified with a visible 'all clear' signal from my nearby village. The signal was the laying of a big red blanket on one corner of the roof of a house. This meant that the village was free of Germans. We had to see the red blanket before we would set off towards the village.

The work by women of watching German movements was not only outrageously risky but almost impossible to imagine; for example, they would be dressed as poor peasants to appear harmless and they would gather horta (wild greens) near enemy bases to spy on the Germans.

Another contribution was to guide commandos on parts of some particular dangerous missions because women would appear less suspicious to approaching Germans.

The role of the shepherds cannot be underestimated. Undercover of their everyday activities they were able to undertake a variety of vital tasks. Because they would roam freely in the mountains, for example, they would detect any suspicious troop movements. They would pass the information along our communication lines. One job that was essential and for which the shepherds were particularly suited was to cover any tracks which were made by our men and armaments. The shepherds would take their animals over the path we had traveled, scuffing out any footprints. They would collect any telltale cigarette butts, or other debris too. The leader of the English resistance forces in Crete, Leigh Fermor, made a speech in Athens in which he said he was going to recommend to his government they bestow medals on the shepherds in Crete.

Above all, the Cretans fed and sustained the whole resistance, using their own resources, everything they could utilize for the cause.

Because the people sacrificed so much for the cause, we, the 'adartes' (resistance fighters) moved in a deliberate manner with caution. We even refused to take some actions which the English requested in order to avoid violent repercussion from the Germans.

To be exact, the English officers I was collaborating with among others, were Leigh Fermor, Tom Dobadin and Alexis Render. They were 'palikaria' (robust young men), with strong enforcing personalities, with administrative qualities and strict to detail to exaggeration point, as they would say: "We have to inflict damage to the enemy no matter what the cost."

They were following the strict rules of the game. They didn't take into consideration the particular circumstances of a given situation, as our peoples' participation in the resistance and the repercussions on them by the Germans.

As an example, I can mention one incident with the English that happened on one of the missions. It was the time the commandos came to destroy the fuel installation at Siva Maleviziou. After completing the mission, when the commandos were ready to get on the boat for the Middle East, Render, the English officer I was cooperating with, said to me that since the commandos were leaving with the boat, it was a good opportunity to seize the Germans at their outpost in Tsoutsouro. Hearing this was a blow for me, because up until then we had carried out our operations right underneath the Germans' noses without their knowing about our missions; nobody yet had betrayed our actions and now we would be betrayed by our own actions. Render said, "I would write letters saying that the commandos had done it, not the local people... even I would force the German guard officer to write a letter saying the same and the Germans naturally won't retaliate."

"I'll tell you it might work if the Germans are thinking like us. We just cannot take a chance like that. There is too much at stake", I answered.

I felt responsible for the peoples' misfortune since it would appear that I agreed to action in the first place. "Besides", I added, "If we took over the guard station manned with only thirteen Germans, the Germans would only replace them later on, so what's the use of taking a chance of causing ruin to the people who support us and jeopardize our operations? All that just to inflict some damage to the Germans?" I said.

He thought about it and agreed with me.

I should mention another but rather humorous incident where I didn't listen to the English. At the beginning of the resistance, whenever the Englishmen and I had to walk long distances on foot, the Englishmen would always ask me how long it would take.

"How long will it take Basil?" they used to ask me.

I would estimate in my mind taking into consideration the terrain and the area, but it would always take us longer. They could not travel as fast - they were unused to the climate and terrain.

They would say: "According to our schedule we have to reach that point at such and such time..."

"Basil, are you a liar? We didn't make the time you said."

"Well... What can I say, some things don't work the way you plan them, I suppose..." I would answer.

"How long will this journey take?" they asked me again, at another time. But this time when making my estimate I added more time.

And that's how it was...

"This is great," one of them said, "We're on time, even ahead of schedule. Good, Basil, you did better this time."

I smiled - but not as they thought in agreement. I had lied alright... this time - they had called me a liar anyhow. I had doubled my real estimate to allow for the slow pace of the Englishmen. There were no more complains from then on.

Also, I had to convince the English of something else. During our long walks, we passed through villages and mountains where there were shepherds who had dogs to watch their flocks because the German occupation had brought some anarchy and stealing.

Wherever we passed through and the dogs barked at us, the shepherds would come out and ask, "Who are you?"

I would go ahead of the Englishmen and identify myself. While the Englishmen stayed behind at a distance I would address the shepherds. I would tell them, "It's Basil and these are Englishmen."

The Englishmen were horrified, "Why did you reveal who we are?" they would ask later.

"Because if I didn't, they wouldn't help us. They must feel they're trusted otherwise they won't bring us any food or look out for Germans, or they might think that we are thieves if they don't see us."

"How do you know they wouldn't betray us?" the Englishmen would say.

"You have to understand, they must feel trusted, besides some of the shepherds are my 'koumbari'."

"What?"

"We Greeks have godfathers as 'koumbari' at baptisms like you English, but we have 'koumbari' at weddings too.

"I don't see it's a guarantee. It's just a relationship."

"What do you mean, no guarantee? The relationship of 'koumbari' is very important to us, it's like our own family and even more. You have to trust me. I trust them."

"Okay, Basil, but this is a measure only of our belief in you."

## BEGINNING OF THE RESISTANCE MOVEMENT

From January 1942 to early 1943 we received weapons, explosives and two rubber rafts. We had to store them for one or two months until the underground forces came from other areas of Crete and took them. Our work at this time was mainly receiving and delivering weapons and getting ourselves organized.

In the beginning I wasn't a leader, I was just a shepherd, a layman, one of the common people. Most of the key positions were taken by military officers, lawyers and doctors. The role of a leader in the resistance was given to me later because of my family and social connections.

Family bonds had been forged in the hard times before the war. Our families, which we revolved around, were the centre of our world. They connected us to our villages and our land. Uncles, aunts and cousins, even distant relations are considered our family which spreads our connections over a wide area. Add to these family relationships the roles of 'koumbari' these unique family loyalties, the starting of life-long experiences, values and commitments through religion, and you could see the extent of our personal network. I was fortunate to have a lot of relatives, a lot of 'koumbari' and friends who helped me during the hard times of resistance. Whenever anything had to be done by the local people I was able to help with my social connections.

For instance, when the English or others in command would ask favours, like getting animals for transportation, sometimes the local people wouldn't cooperate, and I would talk to them and they would get it done. As people in command always had to ask me about arranging these tasks, little by little I rose in the command structure. From starting out as just a courier for the resistance I eventually took command of missions to the Middle East; moreover, I had personal contact with the resistance leaders in Crete.

In retrospect, all our actions in the first year were geared towards maintaining patriotic sentiment among the people, so they would not accommodate the Germans, in other words, not become 'Germanofili' (friends of the Germans). Our greatest accomplishment was to turn the people against the invaders. In order for the

Germans to contain the actions of the Cretans against them, such as sabotaging bases, the Germans had to station thousands and thousands of soldiers here, instead of sending them to the Middle East where they were needed by Rommel.

At the end of 1942 my friend Captain Badouvas and his group left his base camp in Mountain Psyloriti. He told me he thought that resistance forces in our area should not be so widespread. He said that all of us should unite to form one group and have one main hide out in the Lasiotika Mountains. Following his instructions we took between November of 1942 and September 1943 to accomplish this task.

In January 1943, from that new hideout I (at the time still a courier) set out on a mission to take secret correspondence from the Lasiotika Mountains to the village of Aghios Savas to a valley in Kato Mesara. From there it would be sent to the Middle East.

On the night of my journey I had to walk all night through an endless rain storm. It was such a violent storm like rivers of water pouring from the sky, but I struggled on through the darkness and the swampy ground beneath my feet. The rain beat my face as if it was angry with me. Hundreds of trees were tossed like twigs in the wind; some toppled never to rise again, like soldiers giving their last breath for their country. (I heard later that at least 300 olive trees had been uprooted.) I had to go on and deliver my message before the others left for the Middle East.

On my way I had to stop at each village and knock on somebody's door to ask the name of the village. I didn't carry any weapons back then because I had not yet come under suspicion.

I walked all night in the pouring rain, with only lightening to guide me. When thinking that I must be drawing near to Sternes, a bolt of lightening, a sheet of electric fire, rocketed to earth in front of me, like a barrage challenging me to pass through. I swerved from my path and somewhere in front of me a light from the village blinked in welcome. Thinking I had outwitted the elements and arrived at last in Sternes, I headed towards the light, but unfortunately in the confusion of the rain and lightening I had ended up in Aghia Fotia, another village very close to Sternes.

With my overcoat weighing tons I entered the village.

One house had a light on and I went to its door, happy that I didn't have to wake anyone. Coincidently, it seemed, other people wearing khaki uniforms were going to that house too. Although their coats were belted around their waists those resolute dark figures showed military discipline and rigidity. It appeared that they were Greeks - they looked Greek, they spoke Greek. In fact they were Greek deputies assigned by the Germans to keep law and order and officiate in the local affairs.

We stood together at the door while the rain poured down in torrents. As we entered they became furious, and fixing their eyes on me began to accuse me of stealing animals. They said they would arrest me for whoever was out on a night such as this must be up to no good.

I insisted that I had lost some of my animals and was looking for them. This is the excuse we resistance members used whenever we were questioned at night during our expeditions. Even though the house owner said that I wasn't a stranger and that he knew my family, the deputies insisted on taking me in.

Since it was raining, I had the secret papers folded in a handkerchief in my pocket. They searched me fully for knives and guns and wanted me to empty my pockets. Still thinking that I was in Sternes where I had friends I allowed myself to become furious, and to stop them from searching me.

"In my pockets are personal things. You don't have any business looking into them."

Nevertheless they insisted on arresting me, and I said, "Go and ask (so and so) in Sternes about me and they will tell you what kind of a person I am."

Hearing me mention Sternes, they replied, "This is not Sternes. This village is Aghia Fotia!"

'Oh, now I'm in a jam', I thought. I don't know anyone in this place.

In a state of shock my mind raced back to events of the last two days and with them a warning. Two days before I had gone to my village for a baptism in which I was honoured to be the godfather to a child. I say I was honoured because in our culture the godfather is the spiritual guide like a second father to a child for life. It is a commitment.

I can say, these family celebrations were more important for us during the war because they gave us the feeling that our lives had not been disrupted. This baptism was especially important for the child was to be called Niki (meaning 'victory'). There was a special atmosphere at this gathering. Everyone was delighted in calling out the name Niki as we felt to be an act of defiance against our oppressors.

As a godfather I had to take part in preparing the celebration meal. We slaughtered one of my lambs, cooked it in our special way with herbs and spices (I can almost taste it now!). We decorated our house with fine hand embroidered tablecloths, covers and pillows from the 'prikia', the linens the women bring to their new household in marriage.

We laid out tables with our special Cretan food for such occasions loaded with cheese pies 'mizinthropites', cheese cakes, wild greens or 'horta', and our luscious homemade drink 'raki', quite similar to Greece's famous ouzo.

Sitting around our tables we celebrated by eating, clinking our glasses and toasting to health and victory. Conversing and reminiscing led, as it always did at these village gatherings, to singing our ancient ballads, such as 'Risitika' expressing our yearning for freedom – when are we going to breathe freely again – which allowed us for a moment to forget the harsh realities of life under occupation.

Our roaring mood even reached new heights when my friends as always on such occasions joked about me saying 'kai sta dica sou' (the same to you – which meant have a wife and children).

I would respond something like: "What women would put up with so much work to serve you, with my house being like a hotel with you guys," or "You guys scare all the women away," and so on. Even my family would agree. My mother would say on occasions: "Come on Basil, I need help."

We Cretans have a traditional custom – you can say it is a fatalistic custom – to read the future, to find signs about future events such as death, sickness, or danger. To do this we look for signs in the shoulder blade of a lamb. One of my guests who had eaten the shoulder blade of my lamb asked to whom the lamb belonged. When I answered that it belonged to me he looked at me intently as he said, "You must be really careful because you are at the most critical point of your life. You will be in danger. It is as is you have one foot in the grave. Be on guard and really consider carefully any action you take. Beware!"

The deputies took me from the building as I made a last desperate appeal to the man of the house to tell the deputies more about my family. But his daughter, an imposing figure with stern eyes, interrupted me and said, "Now father, mind your own business. Don't get involved in this matter."

Her father shrunk back at this and lost his voice.

Then they took me away. We were now outside the house. Escape would be easy, I thought. The darkness would quickly hide me, the rain is heavy and their weapons are hanging on their backs, but I remembered the warning and stopped short.

"Why are you taking me to the Germans? They will kill me," I complained.

I was about to tell them that they were traitors when they grabbed me and trussed me up.

I knew then that I had lost my chance of escape. If I had been able to escape I was sure that I'd have outrun them. Living in the mountains, sleeping in caves makes one strong, as strong as a wild animal, but remembering the shoulder blade of the lamb and the warning, I stayed calm. Was it because I believed the superstition or because I was taking into consideration the impending danger? Perhaps some superior being is controlling my fate? I felt helpless.

They asked me if I knew anybody in the area. I told them that I knew some people called Agelithakis and Stavroulakis but that they were wanted by the Germans. Then I said I knew someone called Vasilaki Gianni from Charaka, where we were going.

When we reached Charaka we went straight to the coffee shop and had a drink. The deputies shoved a drink in my face but they had to hold it for me as my hands were tied. In the meantime one of the deputies went to find Vasilaki. They returned alone only to say that he was nowhere to be found. We went on to the village of Pyrgo.

On the way undercover of darkness, I thought about getting rid of the secret papers I was carrying, for if I had been caught with them I would certainly have been found guilty. Although I could have thrown them away, I could not bring myself to do it. The papers were like tokens of my conscience and they had to be saved no matter what the cost. I took them from my overcoat pocket to hide them inside the front of my shirt.

After a long exhausting journey we arrived in Pyrgo where the Germans, and the offices of the deputy sheriff, were. I was relieved for I knew that the deputy sheriff was a patriot. All we rebels knew whether the people holding key positions in the city and state government were patriots or pro-Germans.

Finally, at four o' clock in the morning we arrived at the office. The deputies locked me up and left. Even though my clothes were dripping with sweat and I had chills, my only concern was for the secret papers I had with me. What should I do with them, destroy them, or keep them? I decided to open the wax-sealed envelope, take all the papers and put them inside the lining of my coat.

In the morning the deputies came back and I told them that I knew a few people in the town: Elioti, who was with the resistance forces, and a lawyer, his first name Kostas. The deputies returned with the lawyer. who came in reluctantly dragging his feet. He was on guard and hesitated to show he recognised me for he feared that he would be involved by implication.

"His face is known. I've seen his face before," he mumbled.

I could not help saying to him, "Mr. Kosta, why are you saying you don't know my name? Am I not Basil?"

"Oh, yes, of course," he replied.

The deputies cut in saying, "That doesn't count because he didn't say your name".

At this point I decided that if they took me to Sheriff Alexandrou and he decided to hand me over to the Germans, I would tell them who I really was. Then if the sheriff still wanted to hand me over to the Germans, at least the people in the room would hear the whole thing and eventually the rebels would find out and take revenge. You see, I was young and fired with patriotism. I wouldn't let the fear of danger overcome me. Thus I didn't get rid of the papers. After all I was not in real danger yet. Besides that, what would I say to my comrades later? It would be shameful for me to get rid of the secret papers just then.

While I was waiting for Sheriff Alexandrou, I sat by the fireplace in the office contemplating my situation. My hopes rose like the sparks from the fire, when by chance a friend, Stelios, came in. He saw me sitting there and said with a surprised voice, "Hell, Basil, what are you doing here?"

When I had told him why, he began to say good things about me to the others in the room.

At this moment Sheriff Alexandrou came in. His forceful entrance struck me as he drew my friend aside to talk to him privately. I don't know what they discussed, but afterwards the sheriff came up to me, his face sober with paternal severity, and said, "Why do you go out at night? Don't you know that the

Germans could find you and kill you on the spot? Why were you outside when you know it is forbidden?"

Seeing that they were being soft with me, I told them my original story, that I had been out looking for my stolen animals.

He told me to search during the day, not at night. "In any case," he said, "you are free to go."

My friend Stelios must have said the right things about me because as I left, the deputies not only greeted me but also apologized.

"Eh! If you find your animals, come back and tell us," they said laughing.

I left and went to Annavolemata where I was supposed to go to the house of someone named Frangedakis and deliver the secret papers. When I arrived at the house I found only a young boy named George, the son of Frangedakis. When I asked him where his father was and if he would take me to him, he kept making excuses, such as, his father was far away and he didn't know when he would be back, etc. (The resistance was just beginning and people were not as involved as they were to be later on, so they were cautious.) Furthermore, the boy was probably afraid because to him I could even be an agent for the Germans.

During the afternoon a man came to visit. I learned later that he was a military officer, but when we met he wore civilian clothes and pretended to be a black-marketeer. He and the boy knew each other. The man said to me that some of his things were missing and I told him I was looking for sheep.

We smiled and lied to each other.

Time passed by.

The boy couldn't or wouldn't tell me anything worthwhile - like when to expect the people I wanted to see. Neither of them asked me to leave.

Then Kostas Paradisianos came by to see them and was soon followed by Nikos Souris, our translator. He was usually called Telemachos, an assumed name so that the Germans wouldn't be able to identify him. The name had been later changed to Dionysis when our intelligence learned that the Germans had discovered the pseudonym.

I interrupted them: "Are you talking about Telemachos, who is now called Dionysis?"

That was that. They got up and kissed me and became happy.

After a while captain Petrakogeorgis, one of the leaders of the resistance of Crete came, with his son Iraklis, and Leigh Fermor, a solid personality. Leigh Fermor was the English commanding officer of the allied forces in Crete.

As we gathered together, packed like sardines in that small room of the house, with the ceiling dripping from the hard rain outside, I told them about my adventure. While I was talking I was aware of Leigh Fermor's intense gaze. He questioned me closely about my whole ordeal. This marked the beginning of our acquaintance and friendship that extended throughout the resistance.

## THE MISSIONS

My part in the resistance was to assist the missions which were the most important activity of the resistance effort in Crete. On these occasions my group would go to the sea, south to Tsoutsouros, a rugged stretch of isolated coastline, and there under the shadows of the German outposts which were dotted along the coast, we would receive boxes of weapons, ammunition, radar equipment, explosives, or secret papers from the torpedo boat that came from the allied forces in the Middle East.

There was also a constant flow of people coming and leaving Crete. Commandos would arrive on the boats in order to carry out sabotage work on German bases, English officers would come and go from the Middle East from time to time, and other high-level officers would come to contact the resistance. Native Cretans would leave for different reasons: some would leave to avoid German persecution or to enlist in the allied forces there, or to seek medical treatment and even others to continue their education.

Furthermore, we were receiving a constant flow of weapons in case the allies decided to land in Crete for a big showdown with the Germans. In that case, we Cretans would be armed to the teeth to fight alongside our friends.

The boxes we unloaded from the boat sometimes concealed mysterious contents – like one time when we received about one hundred sealed containers in addition to the usual boxes of weapons. These unusual containers were lighter and looked different. What mystery did they contain, we wondered.

We dutifully took them to our hiding place in the mountains and waited for someone to pick them up. We had to wait for a long time. People came, people left, giving passwords for other boxes but nobody seemed to want these.

"Maybe they're meant to be a present for you, Basil," one quipped.

My comrades started to joke in this way as time drew on. Finally, a person sent by the English, who represented the local committee of the city of Heraklion, arrived and gave the password, but it still didn't answer the puzzling question we all had: Why were the boxes so light, and what did they contain?

We had to wait a number of years after the war before learning from one of our former agents what they contained: underground printed material and leaflets. The boxes were light alright but our curiosity was heavy.

Those embarking on the torpedo boat for the Middle East would usually come wearing their best clothes and shoes, so just before the boat sailed we would ask them to undress and give their clothes to the accompanying resistance fighters or guides.

And that's how it was at one time or another; we in the darkness, with the threat of Germans hanging over us, hurrying into the boat and the boat ready to leave...

"Come on you people, we don't have much time, but we're going to have a little fun first. Please take off your clothes!"

They looked at us in bewilderment.

"Are you crazy, are you going nuts?"

Then I would whisper, "What it is, is like you're getting baptized again. Since you're going through water to a freer world you don't need your clothes, but we do; we poor rebels up in the mountains have to fight bitter cold, rain, plus the Germans. What do you think, clothes last for ever? At least it's not our bodies that give out. Thank God! That's why we need replacements. We wear them until we have to shed them - like snakes."

"Don't tell us our underwear too?"

Sometimes women were with us and they would be so shocked that they would say, almost in terror, "Don't tell us to do strip-tease for you!"

"It's for a good cause," we would all say smiling.

"You get all our best clothes and we shiver in the cold? What are you, thieves? What are we going to be covered with?"

"It's all arranged, we have blankets for you."

At another time, there was a priest with us who said "the blankets will be blessed."

"Yes, it will be a second baptism into a new life," I added.

"My mother kept my baptism's," somebody would say.

"Now the second time around you don't need a suit, you just need a blanket... a sacred blanket."

The Englishmen, there to get in touch with the allied command, would always start taking their clothes off first, to set an example for the others to follow.

"See, it's easy, besides, when you get there you will be given new clothes with a new style, so what more do you want? You will get new clothes with all the trimmings, the second time around."

"There," we would say, "only you don't get the koumbari."

"How do you know?" someone wisecracked, "Maybe the Germans would want to be the koumbari if they could see us like that, like phantoms. They would be so mad that they would want to drown us."

"Why?"

"For satisfaction... and to give us our final baptism."

And that's how it was, at one time or another.

My responsibility involved not only protecting and guiding the people who were leaving, but also briefing them on how to behave on the journey to the boat. We had to tell them to be careful not to leave anything behind, not even the smallest object - a cigarette butt in the wrong place could betray our presence. Still people were not careful enough, and on the following mornings I would have to organize local shepherds to erase any tracks we had made, or pick up anything that people might have left behind.

The hardest part of my work was in deciding who could leave Crete. Sometimes ten, twenty, even thirty people would come to my village in the space of a few days to look for me and give reasons or excuses for leaving and implore me to put them on the boat for the Middle East.

Our rendezvous point was usually the same each time - we always chose a deserted stretch of beach. When sometimes we would hear a rumour that the spot had been disclosed to the Germans or had been seen by them we would have to change location. In such cases we would go to the beach at night and with the help of a map and flashlight would find a suitable spot. There we would send a coded message by radio and await instructions as to where the boat would meet us.

On the day of a rendezvous we would arrive at the coast during daytime and hide in a nearby cave until dark, staying almost motionless. At dusk we would ready ourselves to go to the predetermined spot on the beach and wait for the boat. The scheduled arrival time was always eleven o' clock at night.

Luck and weather conditions played a big role in a successful rendezvous, but the biggest danger we faced was that the motor of the approaching boat would be heard at a German outpost. The longer the boat's approach took, especially when sea conditions were unfavourable, the greater the danger.

In some cases the boat couldn't come too close to the shore, so in order for people to go to and fro, they had to lean on something, and that something was invariably me... My job was to stand in the swirling water like a post or a stepping stone giving the people security.

I remember the experience of the sea sucking around me as I helped people or heaved heavy boxes of supplies. The cold, black water filled my boots weighing me down as if they were made of iron. At such times I felt at war, with not only the Germans, but Poseidon, who seemed to be calling me to give up my struggle and sink into his depths. With aching muscles we carried people on our backs to the boat and returned to shore with supplies.

If eleven o'clock passed without a sign of the boat we would begin to despair because the people with us became vulnerable. It would be very dangerous for them to get caught in a skirmish with Germans, and until they were safely on board we would feel as if we were all on Death Row. Not until the following day, when we could go back home to see that the Germans had not discovered our actions and blockaded the surrounding areas, would we feel safe.

Depending on the amount of weapons I was to receive, I would arrange for a number of guides with mules and donkeys to help unload the weapons from the boat, and load them on the animals. I had not only to worry about bringing the right people with me, but also the right animals! The animals had to be strong and sure-footed, not dead-beats. I often had a struggle to find good ones, because not everyone could spare animals for the resistance. Each guide would take responsibility for a particular animal. The guides would load their mules or donkeys and take them to a secret place, such as a cave, where they would unload them and disappear into the night. In the meantime, the other resistance groups would be notified where they could pick up the weapons.

Sometimes we would receive more weapons than we could easily carry. The mules and donkeys would be so overloaded that they could hardly stand, but we had to use all our tricks to keep them on their feet and make them move. They resisted us, and tried to lie down or refused to get up, especially when we would climb steep pathways.

I remember one particular mule which would resist our efforts to make it move by crossing its legs, but we figured a way to cope with that problem: we pushed it to the edge of a ravine, pretending that we were going to push him down. We found that worked with most of the stubborn ones. They would be afraid and stand up. The mules understood; they soon got the message.

One problem was to keep the mules quiet. One night one began to bray and just wouldn't stop. We didn't know what to do. Everyone had a different opinion. Some said to kill him, but that wasn't a solution because the Germans might hear a gunshot or find the dead mule later, and know something 'illegal', in their eyes, had been happening in their self-declared dead-zone.

Everyone gave his opinion, as I said, while we continued to load the animals as fast as we could. Then I heard a man talk angrily to the mule. He said: "You traitor, I'm going to fix you up. You want to betray us. Ha! You'll see."

I was curious and went to ask him what he would do. He said that he would put oil in the mule's butt while holding its tail. From that time on we didn't have any more trouble from them.

Talking about mules, I should tell you another incident that happened on another mission. A guide, his name Vangelis Kariotakis, came from Lasithi with his mule, to take a load of weapons to the resistance in his area. He wrapped them in mats, neatly folded and well covered on the donkey. On the way, he came across a detachment of Germans patrolling the area. They stopped and thoroughly searched him, but ignored the donkey who continued on his way slowly, slowly, as if he was waiting for his guide. What they were looking for was on the donkey, of course.

When I saw my friend next time, to load again, he told me his story and said, "You know, Captain Basil, I guess that the Germans were relatives of my donkey and that's why they didn't search him; they respected him."

On our expeditions through rugged land, climbing steep slopes, traversing great distances and battling nature's elements, a lot of other unpredictable incidents happened, like...

## Taking a Swim

We had been crossing the rugged wild land for hours, under a starless sky, with the dark veil of night enshrouding us. With us were fourteen locals, four Germans and two Italian defectors, and all were going to get the boat for the Middle East. The defectors had stayed with Captain Petrakogeorgis' resistance group until this journey, and were being guarded by some of them now.

It was the heart of winter, and the expedition from Amari to Tsoutsouro was unusually hard. We worried that the hardships of this trek might make the defectors want to return to their own troops.

We, of the resistance, were used to the treacherous climate and able to withstand it, but the defectors were not. They tagged along exhausted, trailing behind like tired children.

The freezing wind beat on us, as our line of straggling men wound along the sides of mountains and through narrow passes. We walked on ground soaked from a recent thunderstorm, which swelled streams and formed lake-like expanses of water in places. We could not avoid stepping into mud puddles and sinking deep into the earth. The stones and dirt, mixed with enervating moisture, rubbed the flesh from our feet, while cold mud seeped into our boots, chilling them.

It was as if the earth was trying to devour us. We looked ahead, through winding valleys across tremendous distances. The mountains, our beloved, imperious mountains where each dent and crevice was like jewel to us, hid the path we travelled. But now these mountains didn't look as beloved as before. They looked stark, threatening, as if they wanted to take revenge on us, for assisting our enemy.

All of a sudden, a frightened voice, not a cool level-headed voice from one of our comrades, but a desperate, tremulous, shrilled voice, a voice of a child, broke the silence of the night.

"I can't go on," the German cried, as he sank into the mud waving his hands in every direction, trying to cling to anything.

His body dropped like a ton of iron splashing us with mud, which further soiled our already worn-out clothes, and made us shiver with cold and pity.

"Look at those pathetic creatures, they can't put up with a little bad weather," said a comrade, Yiannis, mockingly, as he wiped his thick moustache with a large muscular forearm that spread spots of mud from its black mass to his cheek, "Look at the rest of them. They're following with heads down like children looking for treasure."

"What a picture for a girl friend," said George, one of my

comrades, a tall, young 'palikari'.

"Trust you to think of that - you think of nothing else," Yiannis laughed.

"But what girlfriend would look at him now, smothered with mud and pine needles, he looks like a hedgehog," added George.

"Basil, look", one of the Germans pointed to his boots. Our boots are no good... our feet are bleeding."

"Let us... stay here... Don't want to go on," a chorus of child-like men wailed.

"Stay here, stay here," the others joined in.

I couldn't help thinking, 'where are the proud young men in crisp uniforms, pride of their fatherland, now?' These soldiers are no more than helpless children looking to me to save them.

"Look, how they bend to the ground like they want to nail themselves to it," said Yiannis.

"Come on, give me a hand to get him up," I said, in a steady voice.

"We don't have time," someone said.

"I can't, I can't, I can't, the mud makes him slippery. He's slipping from my hand," one of my comrades said, trying to help.

"Easy does it, I'm holding his feet," said Yiannis.

"But the other ones are dropping down. Ah! You're making fun of us, dropping down into the mud to help you, and embrace you..." some Greek voices said.

As we hoisted the people up they just slipped down again like dominoes.

"That's going too far! Come on, get your butts up. Lazy bum, get up!" the big guy, Yiannis, said emphatically.

"Get up, get up," my comrades repeated, and pushed and tugged at them, but slipped too in the process.

I felt sorry for the Germans, but realizing that precious time was passing, desperation transformed my pity to anger.

"Get up!" I shouted.

But they lay prostrate in self pity. Again I felt sorry for the wretches. I looked them straight in the eyes, and showing a comforting face I tried to encourage them, saying with the German words I knew: "It's not too hard, you can make it."

But their expressed response was, "We can't go on. We're exhausted... Our feet are swollen. Look at our shoes, worn out, cracked and caked with mud." And the motion of their bodies pointed to their helplessness and exhaustion. Their hands wavered and shook like leaves, as we pulled them up in the darkness.

They kept falling and sitting. We pulled them up, again and again, in the darkness, in the cold, in the mud, in the unknown, in what seemed to be eternity, for eternity... until they understood that the end was coming closer and closer, and it hit them without mercy.

We pointed our guns at them, touching their bodies, shrunken from fear.

"Get up or we'll kill you," we said.

"Kill us? We... friends... love you... friends."

"Basil, we can't stay here. There are certainly German patrols nearby, the noise," said Yiannis.

"I know, but how do we move them?"

"We must force them to go on," said George with persistance.

"Haven't we already tried that?" I said.

"It's not enough. We can't stay here. If the German patrols come by and hear us, we're in trouble." With that, George poked one of the Germans with the muzzle of his weapon, like he was prodding a stubborn mule.

"Be patient, my friends," I said to them, "They're strong enough to have come to this point, so they are strong enough to go on. Their newfound conscience was built on their country's betrayal of ideals and broken promises. They have seen the light. We praise them for that, and for their action to desert from tyranny, but we failed to realize that they have to fight within themselves, again and again, to ease their conscience. They have betrayed the self respect each man has for himself. The doubt pounds their brains continuously, and is as wearing and exhausting as constant artillery fire, and eventually the body gives up".

I felt the German eyes staring at me at my mouth as I was talking. I wanted to be able to tell them that everything was going to be alright.

"Basil, we have to do something." The voice of one of my comrades brought me back to reality.

"We either leave them or kill them. And your talk of exhaustion is okay, but they've filled their bellies, while I'm hungry," Yiannis said.

"Yes, these Germans... they've been eating like pigs. They should be strong enough. They even stole our food," one of the

Greek people we had with us said.

"Maybe their guilty consciences make them hungry."

"I should be weak, my conscience is not protesting, but my stomach is," Yiannis said.

"Basil, what do you mean, they've seen the truth? Maybe they want to get away from being soldiers. Maybe they are just cowards, and they're not defecting," a worried voice said.

"We don't believe they want to defect. Maybe this is a plot," a chorus of voices responded.

"What do you mean, they behave like that so they can stay here until a German patrol comes by?" a sinister voice said from one of my comrades.

"Let's leave them here, otherwise we're going to miss our rendezvous," some Greek voices said.

"No! No! We can't! They'll betray us to the nearest patrol," worrying voices, coming out of weary faces. "There is no other choice but to kill them," again the same desperate voices said.

The threat of death hung in the air over the very heads of the Germans sitting in the mud at our feet.

"No! No! They are not our enemies now; besides, we can't kill them because of the noise and the bodies."

We had to convince them to go on. Maybe my friends were right. Those Germans only wanted to get away from being soldiers, not that they saw the light. In the end it didn't matter. I had a job to do, to get all these people to the rendezvous point, and I would do whatever was necessary. As my friends were making suggestions and talking, and creating pandemonium, the same conclusion came into my mind. I have a job to do and I'll do whatever was necessary. I stepped forward and pushed my gun into the face of the nearest defector.

"Get up!" I said.

Everyone stop talking.

He looked up eyes clouded with doubt.

"Get up or die here and now!" I said.

There was a moment of complete silence. No one moved. Even the wind had dropped. I kept looking at them intensively, my finger on the trigger, gun pointing. Then, together, slowly at first, they struggled to their feet, and struggled forward. I met their eyes for a moment. I stared at them, and then, "Basil, Basil, see... we will... we will..."

They rose. Our sighs of relief broke the deadly silence, “At last.”

We all went on slowly, but didn’t stop again until we reached the village of Verna, over a muddy, rough, rugged land.

To make sure that the coast was clear I sent ahead one of my comrades to check for any Germans in the village, and indeed they had arrived the previous night. They were staying in some of the houses in the village to inspect the area.

We managed to get in touch with the family we knew, the Vrendithes, who were loyal supporters of the resistance. They led us to a safe place where we could rest and eat. It was an out-of-the way house, a simple Cretan stone country house with a couple of rooms, surrounded by overgrown bushes, like it was trying to mingle with its simple surroundings.

We were given a modest but ample meal that turned out to be a feast. It had some embellishments because of the language barrier. Our friends now, the Germans, enclosed in the house and feeling protected away from the war, were at such ease with themselves that they found their sense of humour. They were relaxed, so between eating olives and ‘feta’ cheese, meat and eggs, they felt the need to talk like chickens, coko, coko, coko... like saying, ‘I’m happy, I’m eating my eggs’, coko, coko, coko! ‘I’m happy, I’m eating corn.’

All of us around the table looking at the Germans mimicking chickens, figured out if this absurdity had to go on it might as well be a contest, as we saw our side the Greeks, to mimic, not chickens this time, but roosters, so we had shouts of “coco” on one side and “ki-ki-ri-kou” on the other.

Each side tried to outdo the other. Yiannis jumped on the chair flapping his arms, and this absurdity went on until others chose another trade, to be shoeshine boys. With their boots in their laps they were cleaning them, rubbing them, pampering them, like they were trying to cheer-up a disappointed, crying child. “Look... look... at my boots,” the Germans and the Italians would say, gesturing, pointing at them.

“Look at the Italian,” one of my comrades said. “He is polishing his boots with oil... That’s why he was saving the oil from the table.”

The other men all of a sudden, turned and stared at the Italian, who, undisturbed, murmured something while he was polishing his boots like crazy.

"Where is he think he is going, to a wedding?" another comrade quipped.

Everybody looked at him, while the Italian continued, undisturbed, murmuring louder and louder, until the murmur resembled a tune, and the tune resembled a loud cry... an aria... La Donna e Mobile...

"First we had chickens and now we have tenors!" George exclaimed.

"What is he singing? I never heard that before," Yiannis said, "It's very impressive."

"Maybe he misses home," I said.

"It's from an opera," George said.

"Why is he singing opera and not something else more... down to earth," Yiannis said.

"Maybe we don't need to be down to earth all the time. Maybe we need to reach something higher... to reach spiritual dimensions once in a while," George said, with a grin.

"Whatever for?" Yiannis responded.

"Maybe to see life in a different spectrum and appreciate... more the spiritual... the philosophical... the arts..." George said.

"Whatever for?" Yiannis said again, but impatiently.

"To keep in touch with our whole selves, not just with the needs of our physical being," George answered.

"And so?" Yiannis insisted.

"Then we would really know ourselves and our capacities, and what we can reach... what heights our potential can reach," George responded.

"Like reaching the stars," I said.

"And overlook the trivia of life," George added.

"Or wars and their miseries..." I completed.

"And the spiritual high is reached when..."

"Oh, George, you're saying this because the war interrupted your studies and you want to preach to us," Yiannis said, while the Italian's voice kept going higher and higher...

"La Dona e..."

"That's what we need now," my comrades said.

"Yeah! A grand finale for now," I said.

After taking a rest, our troops prepared to set out again. Quietly and satisfactory we went on and on through the terrain, that felt more familiar now and more friendly, since we were stuffed to the ears with food and fun. We came to a small stream that glistened under the stars. It wasn't very deep. As I was leading the way, I crossed the stream first and signalled to the others to follow. They stood hesitant at the edge of the stream, moaning and complaining about getting wet, with my friend, his name Psarogeorgis, quavering, "Do you want us to swim across, now?"

"Swim to what, my friend? I don't see any ocean here, only just enough water to wash off the mud and to cool your feet. Maybe I should send somebody to the Germans to bring you a donkey especially for you to ride across."

"Oh Basil! Thank you, but you don't have to. I'll find a way to come across dry."

"Didn't you see the stepping stones?" I asked.

There were some big flat rocks in the stream that had been placed in a row to be used as stepping stones, and I had seen them, but they were so far apart as to make them almost impossible to use.

"I will jump on them one by one and I'm not going to get my shoes wet," he said.

My friend jumped and landed on the first stone. He tried again and landed safely. He shouted to me: "Look at me, Basil, you idiot. I was right. It only takes a little nerve, that's all!"

I said nothing and my friend continued on... but this time instead of landing on the stone he slipped and fell flat on his back in the water with a big splash.

I will never forget his face, as he came out of the stream, dripping wet from head to toe.

"What was it, you said, you didn't want to get your shoes wet, my friend? At least you got your nerve wet. Did you find your nerve while diving?" I quipped.

He was speechless this time, but some others broke the silence, saying, "Oh! He didn't know how to jump well enough, that's why he fell in. We are going to do it right."

And off they went! In a row as if on parade. They jumped over the water gracefully landing on the first rock, looking confident, then into the next one; everything perfect... and then on another, on the fourth, but then they slipped, landing flat on their backs, splashing in the water... taking a swim, with their hands smacking the water in waves as they wanted to punish it for their embarrassment.

I waited on the side of the stream, with damp feet, while they tried to wring as much water as possible from their clothes.

"Can we go now," I asked, "or do you want another swim?"

No one replied.

We continued on, and after a while we came to another area, Metoxi, where there were some old mills. I knew that there was another stream by the old mills, so I warned them to be careful, because at night the stream glittered in such a way that it could easily be mistaken for a road.

I said, "You must cross this stream carefully for it is dangerous. It is full of mud that sticks and sets like cement, and that will give you extra loads to carry, until we can find another stream to wash it off."

This time everyone followed me carefully.

They didn't try to cross it in their own way. They crossed it very cautiously. They followed right behind me like soldiers being inspected. Carefully they crossed watching each individual step, but I noticed a difference; instead of being brave and overconfident, they were cringing and under-confident, and again the same result overtook them. Afraid to take bold steps and to balance themselves, fearing they would slip, they did.

As I stood, waiting for them to wring out their clothes a second time, I wondered at the night's happenings and at what a fragile line we walk. If we rush off recklessly, by ourselves, we often end up in the depths. If we follow someone else too closely the same can happen. It's all a matter of balance.

Finally, we arrived at the beach, but it wasn't the end of our trek. Four times we went down to the sea. The waves were pounding on the beach and the boat was unable to come in close enough. We signalled repeatedly but for three consecutive nights it was the same thing. We stood on the beach, hopelessly signalling again and again, in desperation.

To face the same hardships at the end of the trip made the people weary, exhausted and complaining, but the defectors stayed calm; the worst was over for them.

During the day we stayed motionless in the gullies, stuck in the mountain crevices, wary of Germans patrols in the area. At night we would go down to the sea praying for the boat to come.

"Come on, the bad weather is after us."

"Look at the defectors. They're still calm. I don't see them disturbed," someone said.

"Maybe they brought the bad weather to us, that's why."

"Look at the Italian. He is ready to sing an aria again."

"I wonder why," Yiannis said, "to pacify the sea?" "Or to provoke the sea."

"To provoke the sea?

No, to pacify it."

"To provoke it."

"To pacify it."

"Come on, don't let him, the Germans might hear... Shhh. Keep your voices down, the Germans might hear," voices said.

"And run for their lives..."

"... or bewitched by the true melodic tune."

"Not of 'Pidikto'(a kind of dance), like this," Yiannis retorted, his feet swirling in the air now.

"Come on Yiannis. What's coming over you? Will you dance your way to the Middle East?"

"No, I'm cold, that's all. I'm just trying to warm up my feet."

That's what went on during those four long nights at the sea when it was rough.

Finally on the fourth time it was decided...

"Come on, let him sing. The sea can't be any angrier and the Germans not more aware. Just let him sing a little, just to get it out of his system."

And we let him have a chance to open his mouth wide enough for an "Ah-ah-ah-ah..." when, on the fourth time the sea became quieter, quiet enough for the boat to come close enough to shore to anchor, and we worked feverishly to finish our mission.

But it was a coincidence... The sea has to be quiet sometimes.

Along with some friends of mine were commandos, who landed with the boat, for a sabotage mission, along with many boxes of weapons and explosives.

As with other times when the sea was rough, we had a hard time loading and unloading the boat. Like other times, I was standing in the water, to provide support for the exhausted, desperate people who placed their whole weight on me, as if I were a stepping stone to safety for them. It not only felt like I was lifting half-drowned people, but also I had to resist the current, which tugged at me, trying to devour me and the other helping comrades.

Feeling the pull in every direction, I couldn't help saying to myself, 'By being big hearted, look what a mess you've got yourself into, Basil.'

It was a mess alright, with people splashing in the water, and boxes and boxes of weapons and explosives being dragged through the water. I could not help saying to myself again, 'It's not, 'run for you life', now, Basil. It's 'stand for your life'. Find your strength, find your courage.'

And that's what we strove for, on these exceptional missions; we had no other choice, but to find all remaining strength and courage, and relied on whatever human endurance was left in us.

Finally, we loaded our animals and boxes, that must have weighed about one hundred to one hundred and fifty kilos. The arriving commandos went to Kastelli, and I went back to my base to continue what I had been doing, organizing missions, arranging animals for transportation and whatever was needed at any particular moment.

## In German's Boots

On our way to Siva, to deliver arms and ammunition and get in contact with others in the resistance, we had to go through the village of Plakiotissa that was directly in our path. The people there were friends of mine. They had either enlisted in the resistance or were supporting it.

Plakiotissa was surrounded by gardens and fenced farms, and, with our animals fully loaded with arms and ammunition, we could not avoid passing through. Additionally, there was a festival going on that brought visitors from other areas, and we feared their enthusiasm. It would be impossible to keep the news of the British commandos' presence a secret.

We discussed the situation on our way to Siva with the commandos.

"What are we to do, Basil? Now with us wearing light summer clothing we are visible, even from a distance, and people will recognize us. How are we going to get through the village?" Yiannis said, "The Brits can't pretend to be Greeks and get away with it this time - especially dressed like that."

"Look at his face," he continued, pointing to a young blond-haired commando, his fair skin burned by the summer sun. "Does he look Greek to you, Basil?"

Manolio Bisberakis, one of our guides, looked at him as a brainwave struck him. He stood still, brought his hand up to a salute, and, with his face in elation, he said, "Heil Hitler!"

Yiannis responded almost apologetically, "Excuse me, but how?"

"Pretend my friend... pretend," Manolio said.

He pointed to the red-faced Englishman, "Doesn't he look like a German to you... at least in a quiet street at night after a drink of fiery raki?"

"Oh, you and your tricks, Manolio. Where do you get all your ideas?" my comrades said.

"Survival, my friends," he replied.

"It won't work," one said.

"It must. We'll have to wait outside the village until dark then march in. We will act so well that we scare people, not to their graves, but at least to their houses, and this way they will be out of our way for our good and theirs too," he insisted.

"It's easy for the light-skinned English, but do we look like Germans? How about us being dark and with our moustaches. We are not going to scare them off. We won't be convincing. They'll laugh in our faces," Yiannis said disappointedly.

"Isn't necessity the Mother of Invention?" he replied. "In the dark we won't be so obvious, and if we act confidently people will believe us. Would you dare ask somebody who appears to be a German officer if he was a resistance fighter? We have to act with all the arrogance of the master race. Let's raise our voices practicing our German! Let's have the village deserted," I said with a smile.

And that's how it was.

We waited outside the village until late, polishing our boots, straightening our clothes, adjusting our hats and in a constant play of motion.

Yiannis got enthusiastic. "Come on, let's practice," he said with resolve, as he goose-stepped back and forth.

The English laughed at us, but they all fell in. We practiced until our salutes were perfect. We raised our voices putting a sense of arrogance into everything.

All this happened on a perfect, typical summer night as sweet as the jasmine that filled the air. We smelled the fragrances of spices and barbequed meats that wafted in the air, while the sounds of the cicades were the background percussion to the harmony of content voices. The perfection of the night, with everything so distinct and unforgettable, lifted from us the physical and emotional burdens we carried along our track.

The time had come, and we started rolling into town, cautiously at first, to look even more like Germans trying to catch the village people by surprise. Then, with deliberate manner, like unfolding a military might, we moved in. With our heads high, our hands saluting, our heels clicking we started marching, and barked in German at anyone we met: "Why are you outside this late?"

The people responded in amazement, mumbling incoherently as they would run fast for their lives. And we would shout, "Don't you know there is a curfew?"

Then, people would disappear behind rocks, behind doors - even behind their animals. Yea! I remember Yiannis almost got carried away with his role... He would march forward, his body ramrod straight, his salute crisp and perfect. He would go close to people and in the dark he would look even bigger and more menacing. He scared one man and his donkey so much that while the man froze to his spot with fear, his donkey pulled away from his grasp and bolted home.

How much all men like to be tyrants; that's what I thought when we laughed at the villagers' fear. We had never felt so different. I realized that this sensation was a feeling of power, held within bounds. All of us behave according to norms, but when the possibility of power takes over we behave as if we can conquer a world of new territories we didn't know existed before. In that process we lose touch with ourselves, and we degrade ourselves by oppressing and bringing misery to others.

I looked at Yiannis, and saw how much he had changed in those last few minutes. We all need to be checked, restrained. How must the Germans have felt with such power all the time! No wonder their cruelty seemed to increase. Gradually the feeling passed. I was now on my way - part of the system of checking absolute power. Although we have the potential to be tyrants, the equality of men means that for each tyrant, there is always someone to keep him in check sooner or later.

## The Trap

We unloaded the boat from the Middle East one cold dark night. To transport the weapons and ammunition from it to Kastamonitsa, four to five hours away, we had to form a large convoy. I had some scouts go ahead to detect any Germans if they appeared. This would give the guides more time to unload their animals, hide the weapons and disappear into the night.

We had been travelling in the dark, through rough terrain of gravel and stones, climbing uphill, then downhill when all of a sudden we heard the chilling signal: "Rams… rams!"

A scout returned panting hard and said, "My friend, we're in a trap, we're surrounded."

"Stop where you are," I instructed my guides while I ran ahead to see what was happening.

There, lying behind some large rocks, flat on the ground were my scouts. I dropped down holding my weapon ready, listening for any sound.

"We saw four, perhaps five German figures appear suddenly and then drop to the ground," they said, in low worried voices.

I looked around. It was dark and everything was still. The night was absolutely quiet.

"You must be mistaken. There can't be any Germans around," I said.

"No, no, there are, we definitely saw them," they replied with such an assurance that surprised me. "We saw them," one said again.

"You actually saw Germans? Perhaps you saw ghosts," I said a little sarcastically.

"We saw their shadows, their figures, which dropped to the ground and disappeared," they replied.

We waited motionless and breathless...

"But if there are Germans around, where are they now?" I whispered breaking the silence. "Maybe the Germans you saw are on patrol," I said searching for an answer.

"Perhaps seeing that we were too many for them they decided to hide until they were able to call for reinforcements tomorrow," a scout replied.

The explanation made sense so I told them that in the morning some of us must go ahead and explore the area and if we encountered any Germans we would do what we must do: fight.

Deathly silence prevailed as they considered those words. For me, my chest felt cold as if a bullet had already hit it. We were on Death Row. In front of us were Germans, and around us were more of the enemy blockading our villages. It seemed as if there was no way out.

We didn't encounter anything with our exploration and laid back on the ground. The sounds of the night seemed muzzled while we lingered, waiting for fate to intervene.

'Surely there must be a solution, Basil?' I asked myself. But there came none. My mind was in a vacuum. I didn't know the area well, whether the area had any safe passages through the mountains.

That's it!

What a fool I have been not to think of it before. I didn't know if there were any safe passages.

I asked a guide, "Is there a safe way out of here?"

The guides looked at one another. Then one of them answered, "There is no safe passage through these mountains," but, with a grin that lit his face, he continued, "There is a cave close by, and I tell you what, even though we cannot all hide there, at least we can hide our weapons and supplies."

And that's what we did. We hid the weapons in the cave, and I told the guides to take their animals and leave separately for the nearby villages, where they would spend the rest of the night and the next day, until we discovered what strange things were taking place here. The rest of us would stay behind in the cave, because we didn't want to abandon the weapons completely. We felt responsible for them, no matter what. We also felt we had to confront the Germans if they found us in the cave. I told the guides, if they didn't hear anything, to come back the next night with their animals, to load them again and continue on to our destination.

The guides left and we remained. The night being moonless engulfed us in dread, mystery and fear. We were sleepless listening to every sound, anything that might break the stillness of the night. It was quiet until morning. I crawled out of the cave, and, hiding behind some rocks, scanned the surrounding hillside with my binoculars for any sign of Germans.

Nothing unusual could be seen. Just nature taking its easy, carefree course, tree branches, plump with blossom, weaved softly in the playful breezes; carpets of wild flowers, orchids and anemones, lay in brilliant dawn sunshine.

Peace prevailed throughout the day. In late afternoon a friend from one of the nearby villages came with food, and at night the guides returned with no news.

Feeling safer but puzzled, we continued our journey, and were glad to meet our contacts and finish this mission. After the traditional embraces and kissing, the leader, Yiannis Badouvas, piped up:

"Basil, we almost got killed... You know we left ahead of you, from the boat, and we hadn't gone far when we were forced to change direction," he said. "It was a steep climb. We were marching softly, going as quietly as possible... we didn't even smoke. Then we saw shadows ahead of us. We couldn't hear anything, but they were moving silently and fast. They were searching for someone, and then they hid behind a stone wall. We knew they were there. I think there were only two or three, but I had the impression they were an advance guard," Badouvas added. "So we crawled away, feeling we were under the shadows of death, or more likely death was behind that wall. I could feel it Basil. I couldn't see them, but I could feel them. My gun fused to my hands, but we didn't fight. The hairs on my neck rose. I was sure death was coming closer and closer."

Badouvas was looking over my shoulder, now, his face absolutely serious.

I burst out laughing and he looked up at me as if I had gone mad.

"Meet Mr. Death," I said.

## Strip Tease

It was one of those days. I was busying myself by fixing my shoes and organizing my clothes in the closet - and what a closet, some nails nailed to a piece of wood hung up on the wall. The door rattled and then opened slowly. There he was, standing, full of himself, filling the frame of the door, my friend Andreas.

Wearing a big grin, he said: "I see you're getting ready for the upcoming mission."

"What mission?" I asked.

"The one this week, Basil," Andreas said, sitting down.

"I don't know anything about a mission this week."

"My friend Panos told me there was one," Andreas said.

"You must be mistaken."

"He should know he is going with you, isn't he?" Andreas challenged.

"Mission or not, you're not going. Don't you dare come down to the sea because if you do I'm going to drown you," I said.

'That stupid fool, Panos, would get us all into trouble,' I thought, 'revealing our plans'. Besides I had tried to promote discipline in keeping our missions a complete secret, and what kind of an example would I set if I condone such actions?'

The day of the mission came. Our group went down to the beach and there he was, Andreas, ready, wearing his best clothes and his best grin.

"Don't you dare get in the water and try to jump on the dinghy. If you come near the dinghy I'm going to dump you into the sea," I warned him.

He laughed, but when he saw I was serious the smile faded and he looked hesitant.

The guides who accompanied us on the mission, whispered, "Get ready to jump in the water, get ready, get your clothes off, get ready." Someone said to Andreas, "Jump on the dinghy... get your clothes off first!"

"Basil won't let me," Andreas whimpered.

"He will, he will if you jump fast enough in the water. Get in line behind the other people and he will, he will. Come on."

Eventually they persuaded him and he got undressed. He took his place in line with the other people.

"Good, at last," one of the guides said quickly picking up Andreas' trousers.

"I want his shoes. I want his coat," other guides said.

And the clothes disappeared, flying behind the large rocks, where the guides were hiding. He stood shivering in his underwear behind the other people, who were passing by me using my shoulders to jump into the raft.

On seeing him I couldn't help laughing which turned to anger, as I became furious and pushed him back, while he was smiling impressively at me. Then, I shouted, "How dare you, no."

His face was one of shock.

"If you want to leave, you have to go through the correct procedure," I said, pushing his head under the water. He bounced up and stood still surrounded with foam and bubbles.

"Did you hear me, idiot! Do you think we have these rules for fun! The rules are there to keep everyone safe."

I pushed him under again and held him up.

"Where is your grin now?"

After his... baptism, he headed back to the shore to find the people who had taken his clothes and now were in hiding. What a show for the Germans to see, a half naked man running back and forth on a deserted beach, in the middle of the night, in the middle of winter. 'They would probably feel mercy to have him killed', I thought.

"Come on you guys, give my clothes back, where are you?" Andreas cried.

He became more desperate, running back and forth along the shore calling them, beseeching them, to get his clothes back, and the people playing hide and seek.

"Come out you guys. Basil won't budge. Give my clothes back."

Again no answer, and Andreas sat on the sand, exhausted, almost wailing, saying in final desperation, "How am I going back in the cold with no clothes on? Everyone is going to laugh at me. They would think I've gone crazy."

"Go to Basil to get you a blanket," a voice whispered from behind the rocks.

"Basil won't budge," he said again, looking in my direction only to meet my stern gaze.

"Don't you dare." I was uncompromising.

There he sat, pounding on the sand, pounding and pounding, saying over and over again like a kid, "Basil won't budge. Give my clothes back."

"If you do a striptease you can't expect your clothes back," the guys responded... Ha! Ha! You can't, you can't..."

"Come on, come on."

Ha! Ha!

Then suddenly his clothes appeared, flying through the air in his direction. He scuttled over to them, and as fast as his numbed body allowed, dressed himself and ran off home.

## A Drink of Water Just in Time

One time, I, and a commando, Kimon, who had come from the Middle East, were ordered to undertake a mission to get in contact with some other resistance groups. We had to carry some weapons and explosives with us to an agreed place.

The long walk took us through the village Kasteli, when, walking down the main road, talking and joking, Germans suddenly appeared ahead. We could not avoid one another, it seemed, as they came closer. We had no choice but to keep calm.

"Keep on talking Kimon, don't make any unusual move," I told him. "We're going to pass them with our best smiles."

We passed them, nodded and even greeted them saying "hello."

Turning a corner we were ready to heave sighs of relief, when in front of us appeared a whole garrison of Germans, who were inspecting the area. Suddenly the bags of ammunition hung heavy on my shoulders.

Kimon whispered tremulously, "What do we do now Basil? Just pass them, keep calm again?" he said.

"I don't think we can get away with it twice, my friend," I said, "It's a gamble."

The Germans searched whoever they found suspicious, so one either had to shoot first when they said 'stop', and ran away, or be caught.

"Do we look suspicious?" Kimon asked grinning.

"What do you think?" I said. "Look at us, at our tanned figures as coming from the desert with wrapped-up bulges sticking out of our waistbands and shoulders."

'We had either to continue on, or gamble our fate. But there had to be another solution,' I thought. Looking around, I noted that we were in a neighbourhood of whitewashed houses lining the road. Maybe we should seek refuge in one of those houses.

Kimon and I stood together in the street discussing the situation, pretending to look like friends passing the time of day, then, tried to stroll casually. Surprisingly we were able to keep calm, even though the ammunition we carried cut into our flesh forcing us to pull and adjust it back and forth.

"What if the person opening the door looks afraid or shows surprise," my friend whispered, "or if that person asks us who we are? It might make the Germans suspicious."

'So many 'its' and 'ifs', the heck with it. We are already gambling by being in the resistance, so let's continue gambling, gambling for the unexpected and the absurd,' I thought.

"What else could be more normal for this absurd situation than the person opening the door to see two exhausted dusty guys asking for a drink of water? I said.

"Ha, Ha, the person won't take any negative signals from us," my friend said.

"Only positive signals," I said firmly. "We must appear totally innocent, just poor, tired travellers, looking for a glass of water."

I couldn't stop fingering the bag containing ammunition. It

clinked loudly. I looked around. The Germans were even closer now.

"We must stop patting and adjusting our bundles," Kimon said, with an eye on me but continuing to do it all the same.

"So we must stop fiddling with these bundles. Stop drawing attention to them," I said.

"I can't," he said, "They itch."

"We must smile and look relaxed as though the Germans don't bother us and can't possibly be looking for us, just two innocent, dumb travellers, poor peasants," I said.

"In fact to fool them maybe we have to overact," Kimon replied, "like this." He lifted the heavy bundle that contained ammunition and planted it down then stood up and rubbed his shoulders.

"That's heavy. I feel better," he grinned and winked at me while rubbing his shoulders. "They itch," he said.

"Come on, Kimon. Stop!" I said with impatience. "At least make it so odd and peculiar as to look unsuspicious."

Then with inspiration, he said, "I know, I know... I'll fondle myself. That will go perfect with a dump expression we're supposed to have."

"What do you mean Kimon?" I said curiously.

"This... Basil."

Kimon moves like a crazy man, while picking up the bundles.

"Bravo... What a nerve Kimon, at the tip of their gun. Ha, ha," I said with a laugh. "It's contagious."

Now we were not only flashing sweet smiles, but making faces.

The Germans were coming closer. I was carried away with our dumb smiles. "Eh, Basil, close your mouth," he said, "You look like a dying fish."

"Now the last thing left to do to fool the Germans and our compatriots is to wink our eyes with charm while we knock on somebody's door."

And that's how it was.

The Germans were now a stone's throw away as we chose a door, dropped our bundles on the doorstep and knocked, flushing dump smiles, and nodding in greeting at the officer who brought his patrol to a halt. The ancient door creaked open. An old creased face appeared, more sweet smiles and laughter, while we asked politely for a glass of water. The old face looked from one to the other then ushered us in to the house. We dragged the bundles inside the door which was closed behind us. Behind its wooden planks we heard a click of heels, a bark of an order and the patrol marched off down the road.

In acting like fools we made them fools.

## The Great Potato Hunt

We were traveling with a large convoy on a mission, through wild, untrackable range of mountains, on a goat track. Up and down over the hills we went, seeing spectacular views of crevices and abysses, hanging at the edges of the track. We had been walking over sharp stones and thick bushes and were pricked by spiky plants, all the while feeling the burning heat from the sun and the earth.

The animals we had for our expedition were following us laboriously, carrying rifles, bundles of ammunition, and explosives, heavy on their backs. The bundles of ammunition and explosives swung against the sides of the animals making them struggle and stumble over the steep paths. With the reins over our shoulders, we had to hold the animals along for balance. As we climbed, bathed in sweat, the animals kept shooting glances at us begging for mercy. The animals were dragging their loads more like overloads of arms, ammunition, our personal supplies, and even our transmitter.

The distant fields, shimmering in the sun, looked like crumpled sheets. We could taste the salty earth, as clouds of dust were raised in the dry hot air causing us to breath with difficulty.

"Hot, hot," Tom, one of our English officers, said, sitting down.

Feeling the same way, we stopped. We took off only our helmets. Even our light parachute uniforms, that we had on for camouflage, felt heavy.

"Maybe a breeze will come up. Actually, there are 'meltemia' (blustering breezes) that blow occasionally from the north, out of the Aegean Sea during the summer. Maybe we'll be lucky and they will hit us today," I said grinning. "Come on George, tell them more about our wonderful breezes," I said to our translator. (With his help and with our broken English and their broken Greek we managed good communication with the two Englishmen who were with us.)

"As you know, Crete is between north and south, between

southern Europe and Africa. We have the breezes to cool us in the summer and the south winds from Africa, that even carry grains of sand from Sahara, to warm us in the winter," our translator said.

"I wish we could have had those cool winter breezes, as you said, in some of our previous expeditions. We would have had something to sustain us if we weren't lucky this time, and get some meltemia as you said," the Englishman said.

"Lucky with weather? We'll be lucky if the Germans don't find us," Harry, a 'palikari', who came from the Middle East to prepare for a mission, said. He couldn't but sound sarcastic.

"He's talking about having good weather on expeditions, how about us living in the mountains, sleeping on the ground, exposed to harsh conditions. What can we say? Which is worse for us, being in the heart of the summer, feeling as if we were in a pot, or in the heart of winter, feeling like being in a ice box buffeted by the winds beating us down, and not to mention the rain, the slush, and the splattering of mud!" Yiannis said, touching his moustache.

"Come on it's not so bad. It's a comfort even when it's hot to see the sky reflecting the snowy peaks of the mountains," I said, "like having summer and winter at the same time".

Yiannis looked down. "I suppose that's supposed to be wonderful," he said kicking up clouds of dust.

"But we can still have the caves for comfort, whether it's hot or cold. During the winter there, we gather around fires and feel protected in the caves. We have even found some implements from ancient times and in this way we feel connected to the past."

"And make us to carry on? Hey, Basil!" Panos, completed with an unbashful smile.

"So you're surrounded by treasures, you sleep with treasures," Tom said. "No wonder you feel part of your ancient history."

"And part of modern history, when you think that the Germans might find us and trap us at the entrance," Yannis said grinning.

"They never will," I said.

"Yea! The ancient spirits are protecting us," Harry said with a emphasis.

"Of course," George added... "like the mythical giant who was living in the caves to watch over for unwelcome visitors, where even Dante mentioned in his vision of inferno. Do you know that Yiannis?"

"Who is going to get us out of this inferno?" Yiannis cut in sharply.

"Let's go on," I said.

We started moving along towards the sky, the trees of the lower hills, pines and Cypresses would fade in and out of out view until we saw the white peaks again. The peaks shined brilliantly, white against the tawny gray colours of the slopes. We continue on, our boots hitting clusters of thorns and bushes. Now in front of us, stretched out were thousands of stones, miles of stones of every shape extending down to the mountainside like curtains.

We gazed down. Through the cracks of the stones we could see tree branches peeking out, extending upwards and parallel to the rock seemed as though they were trying to get a foothold.

Yiannis pointed out the trees to the Englishman. "Look at those trees, they're like trying to set a snare, a trap for us, aren't they?"

"You're always trying to see danger lurking everywhere, Yiannis," I said to him.

"Hey, we forgot," our translator said as he turned towards the others who were following behind. "What do we prefer the boiling pot or the ice box?"

"We don't know, it's a hard choice," Tom and the other Englishman said in agreement.

"If it's a hard choice, wait until spring, when the earth blossoms and thousands of wild flowers explode in the fields... whatever you take you find comfort with, it comes like a package deal here in Crete," I said.

"Are you offering us a holiday?" the Englishmen joked.

"Yes, maybe at the end of the war," I said, half serious.

We continue on climbing, a serpent line of men, animals and deadly weapons following behind. We stepped on thorny bushes and clumps of stones, kicking them with our boots while we scratched on the earth's surface.

We then hear some panting. A guide approaches.

"Basil, it's so hot and the animals are so tired that the water won't satisfy them," our guide said through dry lips. "Let's make a stop."

"You say make a stop because you're thirsty, but I'm getting dizzy," Tom said, looking down on the side of the mountains. "Look at those plains, sandwiched between the mountain heights, coming into view."

"They're stadiums," I said with a laugh... "metaphorically of course."

Tom gazed down and said, "no wonder these mountains with their abrupt changes of view and surroundings can influence you in having noble thoughts.'

"Such as to have a 'palikari' attitude," the other Englishman said.

"Were those the kind of thoughts we had when we decided to take this expedition during daytime? Yiannis cut in sharply.

"Never mind about that, we don't have to worry about that for now at least. Instead we have to worry about the people we're supposed to meet to bring us food, and if they're going to be on time," I said.

We climbed through the mountain's winding slopes until we reached a shoulder of a high hill with trees bending over its cliffs. That was the meeting place.

"I hear a strange sound," Yiannis said.

"Maybe it's the sound of the birds flying overhead coming from the mountain peaks, they're taking a dive in the heat to get warm," a guide, who was close by, said.

"Listen, I know this country, I can feel its sounds and pulses but this sound is different, and even if they're the people we're supposed to meet, why haven't they made themselves visible yet..? Say what you want to say, I think they're not the people... they're probably Germans!" Yiannis retorted.

"Yeah! It's a trick, they want to catch us off guard," Panos said.

"Take it easy, fellows," I said, "Let's take a rest here."

We unloaded our animals and pulled our bags containing food to eat and sat under a shadow, but Yiannis, unusual for him, seemed as he had lost his appetite. He looked concerned, "Still worrying about the sound?" I said to him.

"You mean the German sound?" he asked.

"Don't tell me the Germans have detected us and they're waiting until we've finished eating," our translator said with a laugh that was contagious.

"It's the heat. Maybe it's the heat, you're hearing things," we said in chorus to Yiannis.

"Or maybe they like the view from above and they're waiting to get us from there... Ah! ha!" Harry said, pointing to the crest of a higher hill that protruded against the sky.

We went on eating what we had: meat, olives, and our Cretan cheese 'myzithra', all wrapped up in our 'vourlias' (special shepherd bags).

"Basil, you cooked the meat right," the other Englishmen said.

I had prepared the meat the way he liked it. He tucked in his neckline and then he pulled in a nice folded napkin.

"I cooked it right, you eat it right... now we're in a gentleman's agreement," I said.

"Agreement or no agreement, you're a great cook," the other Englishman, the dignified one, said.

"Yeah, a cook and a spy. We should look around for any friends or enemies to make Yiannis happy. But seriously, what is worrying me is why those people are not here yet," I said as I got up going behind some rocks that were in front of me.

The Englishman, the dignified one, got up too.

"I think I see something," he said as he moved towards the rocks that were in front of us.

"Don't tell me that... Yiannis is hearing things, and now it's you seeing things? maybe it's the heat," I said.

"Wait a minute, somebody is coming," he responded, pointing ahead to the curved pathway dropping over the trees. I passed by the Englishman. Indeed, somebody was coming closer and closer. He looked very Greek, but he was wearing khaki boots and pants suggesting he was a foreign soldier. As we were hidden behind the stones, he couldn't see us. We agreed to apprehend him because we were in unknown territory, and we had to find out who he was by force if necessary. He was coming closer and closer to the stones where we were hidden so we popped out and got him. As he saw us armed to the teeth, he was horrified, mumbling strange words. Our translator questioned him right away. The stranger spoke with a unusual Greek accent.

"Who are you?" our translator asked.

"I'm a Cypriot, I came to fight in the battle of Crete," he said with an accent that was distinguishable.

"Where exactly, how, in what particular hills did you fight? And where did the German parachutes land, how did they progress in the lines we fought during the battle of Crete?" that was a barrage of questions from us and exact answers from him.

"After the battle," he replied, "I couldn't get away with the allied ships that came to get us, so the only way to save myself was, instead of running from place to place, to come to the mountains and hide, and I became a shepherd."

Then, he looked around and seeing our large convoy, asked with a tremulous voice, "And who are you?" He didn't know or he didn't realize who we were.

"Don't be afraid. We're the liberation forces."

"You mean in fighting the Germans?" he said. He didn't know.

Then he started to cry and he hugged us. I never forget his excitement when we told him who we were. He didn't know. He even started to sing.

"Here's your bird, Yiannis," George interrupted. "Probably that was the strange sound you heard."

"And you said I was hearing things," Yiannis responded sarcastically.

"Strange things indeed," the other Englishman, the dignified one, completed.

"What are we going to do next, Basil?"

"Are we going to wait for those people to come or to continue on? Why aren't they here yet?" the guides asked.

"Maybe they got caught up with the 'panygire' (picnic festivity) down in the Lasithi plain," I said jokingly.

"I can tell you, if you go there, you'll forget everything," Yiannis said. "Do you remember, Basil, three years ago when we went to the panygire?"

"What is a panygire?" Tom interrupted.

"A picnic celebration."

"What kind of celebration is it? What's the occasion?" Tom said.

"For this particular panygire, every year people gather to buy potatoes when the potato crop is out. Picture this," I said, "people come from all over the countryside to get together, to drink coffee or cook food over wood fires, and have fun hoping to get a plethora of potatoes.

"And don't forget people dance, Basil," Yiannis said.

"How could I forget the dancing, Yiannis? Whenever I saw you there, you were on the lead and you had all the action, most of the time."

"What do you mean he hal the lead?" both Englishmen asked, "and what do you mean he had all the action? What action?"

"You see, we dance in circles and the one who leads does all the extra action of whirling and swirling and heel slapping until he gets tired or until somebody else jumps in... but nobody could cut in and take the lead from you, Yiannis... who would dare? You were the star."

"Ha! Ha! Ha!"

"So if the Germans appear, that's what you have to do, Yiannis... dance your way to the stars. Nobody will interrupt you for sure, so why are you worrying?" Panos teased.

"Well for now we just have to settle by stepping on thorny bushes, kicking them with our boots and feeling the hard earth," Yiannis said with some kind of disappointment, as he lurched ahead.

"I can say one thing," the Englishman, said, "I've captured the whole picture of the way it was."

"Maybe he captured a picture of your 'kefi'," (high spirits), I said to Yannis.

"I don't have any kefi now," Yiannis answered.

"But, you're plowing ahead. What's the rush?"

"Maybe he wants to go down there now while that panygire is still going on," Panos quickly cut in.

"Oh yeah! How do you know?"

"Because you're kicking your boots harder. Or... maybe you want to see Lasithi first."

"Look at those windmills, way down there," one of the Englishmen said. "There must be thousands of them," the same Englishman, the dignified one, said. "They look like huge flowers... why so many?"

"For the potatoes."

"Potatoes?" The Englishmen looked surprised.

"Yes, the area is famous for its potatoes."

The descent became more abrupt. The line of animals grew more unsteady. Some animals began slipping.

"Hey! Come on! Help me with my animal," one of the guides said. "It's carrying the transmitter."

"Easy does it," we said as we ran to hold the animal, but to no avail.

"Maybe he's a selfish donkey," Yiannis said, while pushing the donkey off the edge of the ravine and the donkey still slipping again and again.

"Where is he trying to go?"

"Maybe he's trying to go to a cave down there because he knows how cool it is there," a guide said, laughing.

"Ha! Ha!... maybe he knows a faster way to get there than you, Yiannis," Panos quipped.

The animal was pulled back from the edge of the ravine.

"Come on, you guys, we should keep a closer check on our animals," I pointed to the guides.

"Yeah," Yiannis agreed. "Imagine the transmitter slipping off going down and down and up on one of those windmills and be swirled around and around... and be dropped at the lap of the Germans like being a gift of the gods.

"And we would make history," Harry interrupted... "ancient history."

"Oh, Yiannis, you're not only hearing and smelling things, but now you're imagining things," we said in chorus.

"Well, let's go, the heat is getting to us", I said.

Yiannis continued on undisturbed. "Imagine if it were March, when the sails of the windmills are packed away and when it's windy, with the windmills whirling and spinning their iron wires making wildy metallic noises like groaning in agony... beaten by the wind... and it would be like sending radio signals to the whole world, not just to the Middle East."

"Of course, that could happen if it were March," I couldn't help saying,

"Hey! Take a hold of that. Who has the imagination now, Basil?" Yiannis said with a winning smile.

"Maybe because I'm worrying about what happened to the people we're supposed to meet. Let's go! The heat got us all," I said. "Farther down it will be more comfortable, it will be a relief."

"How?" Tom asked.

"You'll see."

We descended some more. Then the Englishman said, "I can feel some change in the air..."

It was like getting away from bushes and shrubs... only trees, blossoming trees, apple groves, and plants, any shape of plants coming into view, like coming from a tropical island.

"Where are we? In the tropics?" Tom asked.

"Don't tell me you see waterfalls, too," the other Englishman said smiling.

"I don't know, but look at those white lines that look like little rivers running down," Tom answered.

"It could be an extension of the snow from the mountain peaks melting away, adding to the picture," I said laughing.

"So fast?"

"Yea."

"I hear rustling of leaves, of bushes, voices cracking, Basil," Yiannis said, as he was following behind me.

"Again, Yiannis? You never quit," I said...

And then, "pssst, pssst, Basil, here I am."

"Who is there?"

"Me... here I am," said one of our guides, lent to help the people we were supposed to meet, as he appeared into view from a small pathway on the side of us.

"Hello, Manolio," Yiannis replied. "Here are our people! Once again I was right."

"But they're not Germans," I responded.

"Oh, well, you can't win them all." he said, with a settling tone.

I looked around, but nobody else was coming with him.

"What happened to the others?" I asked Manolio.

"They got caught!"

"They got caught!" everybody in chorus.

"Yea... in the panygire, catching up with friends, eating and celebrating, too tired to come... so they sent me alone... they said I can walk a lot faster than them and I know the area better than they do, so here I am, ahead of you," Manolio said.

"How is the situation? What's going on in the panygire? Why so late," I asked Manolio.

"I have good news! The Germans are in full speed. Their operation is full success. All their stations and communications are intact and busy with keeping everybody away from smuggling potatoes that the Germans want for themselves. All their troops are there guarding every pass, every road, every intersection going in and out of the plain. They're so busy with detecting any smuggling of potatoes that they don't stand a chance to detect you... or these potatoes," he said. "These are some of the unearthed ones that would come up later," he said as he pulled out a couple of potatoes hidden in his cap.

We continued on with a more pleasant atmosphere surrounding us. It was not that hot any more. The changes of our climate worked for us in the end... and if you like to know, our operation too, was a full success!

That's when we changed base to a different locale in another range of mountains while watching German movements prior to the abduction of Kreiper.

## ESCAPE OF THE ITALIAN MAJOR CARTA

I was told by the British that our upcoming mission was very important. We had to help an Italian officer, Major Carta, who had been the leader of one German sector of Crete, to defect.

While we were waiting for him, we learned that the Germans had slaughtered hundreds of villagers in Vianno, a mountain village, in retaliation for Germans killed in a clash with resistance fighters at Symi. The Germans took four hundred and fifty people from fourteen villages and executed everyone. It was one of the bleakest moments of the occupation in Crete, but it didn't thwart our spirit, our devotion to the cause for the liberty of our people.

Tom Dobadin, the English commanding officer who was collaborating with us, arranged for Carta to escape through Tsoutsouro where I was waiting. On the 20th September, 1943, Carta arrived at Tsoutsouro along with his staff of four. From Tsoutsouro we made radio contact with the Middle East and arranged to meet a torpedo boat the next day.

To my surprise Captain Badouvas and thirty co-fighters, arrived at the coast wanting to leave on the same torpedo boat because of a disagreement he had with another resistance group. I don't exactly know what had happened and why they wanted to leave. When I had left them in the mountains they had been united and there had been no political dissension. Probably it was the beginning of political disagreements within our forces.

However, that was no reason for us not to be in camaraderie with one another. Having on our side the Italian major was a boost for us and feeling that we were on the winning side we had a party before going down to the beach. We had a good time. We ate, drank to good health, good luck and victory and sang our ballads.

Furthermore, I had an occasion to let them taste a sample of my cooking; I cooked the meat. Carta kept congratulating me on my cooking. My friends joked about when I was going to get married and if I would ever find the time or opportunity to do so; even the English officers as Leigh delightfully agreed to the jokes about my marital status. With all that, the night had been unforgettable.

In the meantime the Germans, having learned of the defection, mobilized their troops to find Carta. This caused great anxiety among Cretans who feared a widespread spiteful backlash from the enemy occupiers.

This mission was the toughest so far, for this time the chances of a clash with them were greater. It was bad enough to get caught with a group of other Greeks, but it would be much worse to be caught in the company of Italians or commandos. The desertion of their allies and the presence of commandos in Crete bothered the Germans and angered them. For these reasons the reprisals would be far greater than anything so far.

Hence, the Germans mobilized everything they could in order to catch Carta. They dropped fliers from planes promising a big reward for his capture, dead or alive. Every sound was threatening to us. With each plane flying overhead we hit the ground flat and immobile.

I remember the times Carta looked terrified as he read the fliers that had been carried to us by a mischievous wind. As we were stuck to the ground, under the shadows of the planes overhead, Carta kept looking at us, looking at our rugged clothes or at our wild unkempt beards while saying to Leigh Fermor, "What has any one of them to lose by turning me in for the reward?"

With a sober face, Leigh Fermor assured him over and over again by saying, "These people are not here for the reward, not even if the whole of Italy was offered to them would they consider doing a thing like that."

Then we set out for the last stage of our mission: the journey to the beach. Because Carta could not walk easily in the night darkness, we had him ride a mule. The area was barren with big rocks and steep cliffs, with few trees or bushes for cover. Later we stopped to rest, hiding our mule under a tree and ourselves in a cave. We were near Tsoutsouro.

For two days we hid in the cave waiting for our boat to arrive and listened for the slightest sound. The hours passed slowly and although we tried to make conversation each of us felt that gnawing fear in the pit of our stomachs. The darkness and dirt of the cave made the waiting worse - but we at least were more used to it than the Italians, who moved restlessly hating the enforced inactivity.

We set a guard outside. Some time passed. Suddenly the guard shouted: "Germans!"

"How many?" I asked.

"Four or five," he replied.

My first thought was that a German patrol must have seen us. I tried to tell the guard not to move, to stay motionless on the ground but he kept saying, "Eh, what?" as he moved from place to place.

The Germans were accompanied with a Greek deputy. I knew him. His name was Marino, and he was our friend: he was Greek at heart. As they went to get a drink of water they saw the mule, which they obviously found suspicious since they were in a German-declared dead zone which meant that no one but Germans were allowed.

Marino hurried ahead as if to scout the area. He knew some resistance fighters were probably nearby and wanted to warn us. The Germans took the mule and approached the place where we were hiding. Suddenly the slaughter of Vianno raced through my mind and I thought how easily it could happen again, that more people would be killed in reprisals and I felt responsible for it. I didn't want it to happen as I felt a strong compassion for my people, for my country.

The distance between the Germans and us narrowed. It seemed as if we had no choice but to shoot. Hands tense, guns levelled, we prepared to fire. But just then the Greek deputy popped up by a stone wall directly in front of us and whispered, "The Germans probably saw you but keep down."

Badouvas said, "Tell them to come closer so none of them can get away."

We had given the Germans as much time as we could to avoid shooting but they were coming dangerously close. With apparently no choice we aimed, waiting for my command, to shoot...

Suddenly, a tune split the air: one of the Germans began whistling. Then Marino winked at us and picked up the tune and turned around. We breathed great sighs of relief and lowered our weapons to the ground. Marino joined them as they turned back.

Did they know we were there? we wondered. I remarked that if they had suspected something and were returning to call a guard station for reinforcements, we would still be able to complete our mission. Only those who had to stay behind might face danger.

During the night we set off to the sea to meet the boat, but the weather was miserable and the sea rough. Every time I went on a mission I felt as if I was carrying the weight of the whole mount Psyloriti. A successful mission spared whole villages from ruin by

German retaliations. Of course, we who conducted missions could escape if we clashed with Germans, but more importantly, if we were not detected we could continue our operations. Nothing on our missions, whether it was walking all night or traversing dangerous pathways and gullies, bothered me as much as waiting for the boat. We would lie in agony waiting for the sound of its approach at eleven o'clock. I swear my heart stopped on such occasions.

That night as usual we listened for the sound of the boat. Eleven o' clock arrived with the sound of a boat, then... silence. We strained for the sound again. It came but faded until we could scarcely hear the moan of its engine over the murmur of the agitated sea. It was too rough for the vessel to approach easily. This coast at the best of times was difficult, but this night the foaming, crashing waves battered the shore with deadly ferocity making our attempts to meet seemingly impossible.

We agonized that sparks from the boat's engine, brilliant in the darkness, were visible for miles; however, although the elements fought the boat, the roaring sea also protected it by drowning the noise of its engine. For a moment the boat leapt on the waves ready to be devoured by the rocks standing threateningly baring their dreadful teeth.

When for an instant the boat looked as if it would be crushed on the rocks someone aboard shouted, "Stop! Turn off the engine."

The anchor dropped and the motor stilled as the vessel lurched and heaved as if wanting to tear up the very sea bed its anchor had impaled. It drifted close to land now as rafts were dropped over its side into the black water.

Some Englishmen jumped into the sea catching a rope which was tossed to them. They tied one end to a raft. Another was grasped by us on shore and tied to a rock on the beach holding the raft to make it easier for the people to get in. Other rafts were held likewise.

The first to get into a raft was Carta, but as other people climbed onto other rafts I heard a shout. "The rafts have broken loose!"

In a frenzy people swam towards the boat, but some could not make it. Panic and fear for survival started to overtake the people. Worried, looking around in confusion seeking for somebody to blame for their predicament they complained with voices full of despair. Accusations flew in the winds. "The crafts were broken on purpose!"

"We can't all swim, you didn't want to help all of us to go abroad."

"We're only poor Greeks, not Italian generals."

The boat left with those who were able to clamber aboard. We who were left on the beach hurried back among the rocks to hide.

Overwhelmed by what they said, I told Tom Dobadin in broken English, "Mister Tom, we have over twenty people who will have to return to their villages. Once that happens all will know what we are doing and where our rendezvous point is. Furthermore, the Germans may find out endangering our future missions. We must keep everyone here and send a radio signal for a boat to return in two or three days to pick them up. We cannot let them go home."

He agreed with me and we made plans to stay nearby.

At dawn, Tom gave me a coded message to radio, but the allies had broken off contact. I pleaded with them to answer me and eventually they did. They told me that although Carta had arrived in the Middle East, the Germans had seen him leave and had begun to patrol all the southern coastline. They said that missions from the same spot would be too dangerous and that we must change to another rendezvous area towards the western part of Crete. They suggested Rodakino.

Tom and the others immediately left for that place. As for me, I took the English officer Render and some others and left for my village. Later I discovered that the Germans intercepted a number of those who were on their way to Rodakino. Many of them were killed and Rodakino was burned in retaliation.

Crete paid a price for Carta's defection by suffering the consequences, but this didn't have an affect on peoples' devotion to the cause of freedom as they continued on with their resistance.

## THE RESISTANCE SPREADS

In 1943 the resistance took on larger proportions and had become organized. In the summer of this year, Captains Badouvas and Podias – two of the leaders of the resistance in Crete – called for me to go with them to the Lasiotika Mountains to meet English commandos returning from a search-and-destroy mission of fuel installations at German airfields near Casteli and Terraki. Allied forces commandos undertook such forms of sabotage frequently in order to obstruct German expeditions and bombardments.

This time John Badouvas and I were to meet the commandos and lead them to a rendezvous spot nearby a village called Aghios Savas. The commandos who could not make it to the first rendezvous would continue on to a second rendezvous point close to Aghios Nicholas, and from there would leave by boat for the Middle East. The group was made up of one Greek commando, Kimon Zografakis and five others.

On our way to Aghios Savas, John Badouvas and I talked to the commandos. Seeing they were well armed but leaving Crete, we asked for their weapons.

"Why do you want to take all the guns to North Africa? We need some here. Give them to us and we will fight!"

"We'll give them to you, but not now," they said.

They had five machine guns and five other weapons.

Our long trek, through rugged terrain of rocks and loose stones that reflected the heat of the burning sun, was only made with great difficulty and perseverance. It was a heat wave. It affected Captain Badouvas as such that he was not able to walk the full distance to Aghios Nicholas, so we left him behind. And despite heat, cold, rough terrain or great distance, it was imperative that we always arrived on time during such missions. I took a guide named Lichico with me who knew the area very well.

I told my translator, Nick Souris, a serious man and one of the most devoted to the resistance, to remind them that when the mission was finished, the commando leader should give us their weapons. The leader said, "I'm going to give them to you when we leave, because something may happen, like a skirmish with the

Germans."

"Okay," I said, "You can give them to me when you embark."

I knew that having the guns would give me a problem which would have to be resolved. The beach and that particular place was unfamiliar to me and I didn't know anyone who could help me carry the weapons back to the mountains to hide them.

An idea struck me that perhaps I could ask some of the Greeks who were going to depart with the commandos to stay.

I turned to one. "What are you going to do in the Middle East?" I asked. "There is a resistance here. Here is where you are needed."

"The Germans are after me. They're prosecuting me," a young man replied.

Another one told me his brother had been killed and that the Germans were now after him. A third said, with a chill in his voice,

"The Germans are after our whole family. They're going to kill us all."

"We'll hide and protect you," I said. "We in the resistance are not afraid of anybody. We can give you protection. If you leave you're not contributing anything to your country."

"I want to fight for the allied cause there," another young man said, his eyes seemed to be fired with anger.

"You can stay. It's just the same to fight here or there. We can use the weapons to fight for our cause here in your country as in the Middle East. But without weapons we cannot fight, and first these weapons must be carried and hidden fast. If they are found by the Germans it would be a lethal blow to your brothers and sisters here. Here is your opportunity to help our country."

I talked at length to them with zeal and in the end I persuaded some to stay behind and help.

Although we were unaware of it at the time, the Germans had killed fifty people in retaliation for the burning of the air fields and had increased the number of patrols in southern Crete to intercept us. We did know that they were after us because when we were passing through the valley of Kato Messaras near Aghios Savas, patrols passed us numerous times, but didn't see us.

We would hide motionless in the gullies almost not daring to breath. At other times we would cling to wild branches, pressing ourselves into the cliffs. Rocks and spiky shrubs pricked and scratched us but we lay immobile, listening to every little sound.

It was not that we were afraid to kill or be killed, but we did fear

German retaliations. A whole village or a whole region could be destroyed; consequently, it was imperative for us to watch and avoid any confrontation with the Germans.

It was a beautiful fresh morning about six o' clock as we took some well deserved rest in a trench behind the crest of a hill. The only sounds were those of birds, animals and the rustling of trees in the gentle breezes. We laughed and joked as if all was peaceful. The war seemed far away and time stood still...

"Rams! Rams! The rams are coming," a guard's voice cried out.

We scrambled.

I was far from where I had left my gun while I had been talking and joking with the English. I grabbed one of the commandos' guns from the ground. Together with Souris and the others we encircled the Germans to trap them.

We caught two very quickly, but how many others were there? In the confusion it was impossible to see beyond the area of immediate action.

"There were three," someone shouted.

A second said that one was escaping. We set off in pursuit. I scrambled down to a place from which I could have a commanding view of the length of a ravine. Ducking and weaving I ran towards its rushing stream.

Close to the stream, now, I heard gunfire from my south, upstream. Running, splashing, I crossed it, leaping to the top of its other bank. The sun temporarily blinded me.

I ran forward but the sun had now appeared over the tops of the mountains blinding me again. Someone began to shoot at me. Squinting I tried to make out who it was but I couldn't see anything. The person must be ten meters away across the stream, I thought.

A bullet whistled between my legs. The shooter was close by and coming at me but shielded by the dazzling sun. Another shot. I raised my hand to my eyes, trying to see him. I was terrified and confused.

Was death playing jokes on me? Provoking me to what response? An act of cowardice, or courage, or even of defiance? I didn't know who was shooting at me. Perhaps he was English thinking of me as the enemy because of the Italian shirt I was wearing. I raised my hand and shouted, "No! Greek.! Don't shoot!"

Then I saw a soldier wearing a German uniform. He was reloading his gun. Were there more, I wondered. I dropped for cover. My situation was terrible, between life and death. If I lived it would only be due to God's Will because we were close enough to have split a cigarette between us.

I turned and ran, terrified with my head down, towards the stream. Tripping at the bank I went down with a splash. The cold water swirled around me as if trying to pull me to the bottom of its watery grave. My clothes and boots helped to hold me down and I stayed under until I couldn't any more.

I saw some rocks protruding from the steam forming good cover, and I waded over to hide. Shots rang out and bullets ricocheted off their smooth surfaces making pinging sounds.

Then I realized that just as the sun had blinded me it must now be blinding him; furthermore, he must be alone, but if that is so why is he so composed? It must mean that I am surrounded. My mind began to race beyond my control as I struggled away through the stream. Was there any hope? Was surrender the only option left for me now? Should I slink away like a frightened animal? All choices seemed shameful.

Suddenly, the German took up his gun, shouldered it as a hunter would after finishing his day's hunting, and walked slowly away downstream. I still had the English gun not knowing how to handle it but thinking I would give it a try, I figured, I had to stop him before he was able to get reinforcements. I was now under cover and could shoot him easily if I had a weapon I knew.

Composing myself, I took aim at him and pulled the trigger... nothing. Again I tried but to no avail. I didn't know then that its bullets were not ready to be released because they were not chambered like an ordinary pistol. I didn't know that I had to pull a bolt first. Instead I pulled the trigger again and again but it didn't fire.

"Ah!" I said in frustration slapping it. "Ah... ah!" I shouted. "Come on. Come on!"

At that moment, an Englishman named Lasser approached. He was a big man, with eyes shaded by heavy brows. In his large hands he held a rifle. From where Lasser was hiding, he gesticulated to show me how to ready the gun for firing, but I could not see him clearly as bushes were in the way, just his lips moving. He pointed impatiently for me to shoot the German who was now walking unconcernedly away.

I said, "It's no good. It's not working." He came closer to show me but I said, "It's useless."

'Oh, what is the matter with me,' I thought. I could only fumble with the gun. I could not even follow the simplest instructions.

By now the enemy had disappeared from view.

We started to run in his direction. Suddenly a young shepherd boy sprang up from his hiding place pointing and shouting, "There! He's over there," pointing in the direction of the German.

I was now on the west side of the stream and the boy was high up on the other side. I came out from under cover and saw that the German had not turned back towards his base, perhaps because he had heard the boy taunt him with the words, "Just a minute, son of a bitch."

A machine gun has two triggers: one fires a burst of bullets and the other fires single shots, just like an ordinary gun. Instead of shooting a burst, I shot one or two shells but both missed. I saw him readying to shoot again.

Seeing Haradikakis, one of our comrades, coming up with Lasser, I pointed for them to go around to the other side and catch the German alive because the boy had set him up. However, instead of doing so, Lasser, now angry, waved and said, "No, no, no, let's leave."

I couldn't understand why. But Lasser, clearly upset insisted, "No! No! No!"

I ran over to him and to our translator. "Come on," I said, "He's a sitting target."

"No!" Lasser said insistently.

Souris spoke to him quickly.

"Basil, we have to leave now," Souris said, "Lasser insists."

"We have him set up," I replied, "He'll go for reinforcements if we let him go."

Souris translated for Lasser.

"He says we have to leave or we won't make the rendezvous in time and if we leave now, reinforcements will be too late."

"But if we catch him we'll have plenty of time," I countered, "If the boat is late you'll get caught."

Lasser became calm but hesitant. He was silent for a minute then said with a steady voice, "No, we must leave now. First we must send a signal to the boat and they will be on time. Any reinforcements will be late so we must let him go."

As it was the boat did arrive on time. Lasser caught it with the other Englishmen and left. We Greeks remained to debate our strategy and share our worries.

"It's not safe to go back," one said, "Perhaps we should lay low for a while."

We all agreed that the Germans would soon be scouting the area for us.

"There will be Germans crawling everywhere," another said desperately.

"So it's better to leave this region," I said.

"How will we avoid the German road checks?" one asked.

"How many know the area well? They can't block all the goat tracks," I replied, "We should split into small groups. We will appear less suspicious that way."

It was decided and we hugged and kissed one another and departed.

"Goodbye, good luck," we wished one another.

My immediate problem was what to do with the guns. "I don't know the area," I said, "Where can we hide the guns?"

"I know a good place," said my friend Vardis, "near Kato Mesara at the foot of the mountains.

Our group was five: Vardis, Nick our translator, two others and myself. We spent the first night on the plain at Kato Mesara and the following night headed towards Psyloriti mountain. This mountain held the best hiding places with its rugged slopes and rocky terrain offering us refuge that would make us feel enclosed in the safety of Mother Earth.

As we climbed its rugged flanks, its solidity underfoot buoyed us giving courage to us all. We told one another that we would not die. If we met Germans we would fight to our dying breath. We would never give up.

On our way we were able to locate telephone wires used by the guard stations to communicate with each other and cut them. Souris wrote and tied a note to the wire. It read: "Cowards. You are the worst army in the world. Why do you retaliate against innocent citizens? We will destroy you for that."

He wrote it in English and signed it with an imaginary name and on the reverse side he wrote the name of captain Badouvas, a heroic Cretan freedom fighter the Germans feared.

We reached the village of Anavolemata which was in a near state of panic. People had gathered outside their houses, on street corners, at 'kafeneon' (coffee shop) tables. One could almost taste the fear. The villagers, whom we did not know, looked at us suspiciously. No one would talk to us. They acted as if we carried danger in our pockets.

Trying to appear nonchalant, we walked slowly through the square, turned the corner of the coffee shop and found a hiding place close enough to hear their voices.

"Where is the blockade?" one was asking.

"Are they coming here?" a woman questioned with a worried face, "What will they do to us?"

If we had been discovered, we might have been reported. What were we to do now? If I hid at Psylóriti mountain, I would be away for at least ten days and no one, particularly my family would know anything about me. They would assume I was dead because of our fight with the Germans. And what would they do, my family and the wife and children of my good friend Badouvas? (the brother of the leader Badouvas)

I became worried thinking about this. They would probably feel abandoned to their fate and leave the house and scatter. I made a decision right there behind the coffee shop. I would go back home. The others responded upon hearing this with bewilderment and surprise, "What did you say? You cannot leave."

The love we had for one another cannot be explained in words.

"Basil, you can't go home now. All the places are surrounded. You'll surely get caught."

They tried everything they could to get me to change my mind but to no avail. In the end they just hugged and kissed me and we wished one another luck.

Vardis spoke up, "Wherever you go, I'll go."

That was that. Vardis and I departed while the others left for the mountain. We didn't know if we would ever see one another again.

Our route led us through a region, west of Asterousia mountains, that was patrolled by about three thousand soldiers. Asterousia was a mountain chain rising from the large valley of Mesara in the vicinity of Aghios Savas in the form of a ring. I was dependent on Vardis because I didn't know very well this section of the mountains. We made it safely through the blockade.

I told Vardis that we should travel only under cover of darkness but he objected. He also wanted to visit his family who lived nearby.

He kept saying, "I know a safe place to hide. Don't you worry. I cannot go on without seeing my parents."

We did as he desired and reached the village of Hale. The hot days of summer were here and we were hot, hungry and thirsty, so we stopped to eat what we had with us - a can of American bacon. Need I say that the salty food made us so thirsty we could not stand it? But we gratefully ate and slept.

Next morning we found water and Vardis left me in order to see if the Germans had made any reprisals against the locals; not far from where he left me, he saw Germans and had to hide.

Meanwhile, I sat hidden in a deep gully behind a clump of wild shrubs with my machine gun on the ground and waited for him to return. I had no idea where I was, I was isolated. I felt like a stone that had been thrown wildly to the bottom of the world, in its solemn emptiness.

One hour passed. I was so thirsty that I counted the minutes like an Englishman, and I looked to the horizon in desperation. It shouldn't have taken him so long because it would not have taken him more than half an hour to reach his destination, I thought to myself. I lay on my back and looked at the surrounding mountain peaks that seemed to hold the weight of the sky.

Then I heard voices from the other side of a big rock in front of me. I crawled forwards. Suddenly shadows fell across me like shadows of death. I turned and looked into the barrels of four German guns. My mouth dried up totally.

"Come on, come on!" one growled, "Who are you?"

I knew I had my identification card on me and fortunately my weapon was a few metres away out of sight.

"Greko, Greko... steal goats," I said in faltering German.

"Paper!" he commanded, gun still pointing, finger on trigger. I slowly, carefully, passed him the identification card trying to appear relaxed.

They seemed to take ages to inspect it. Then they shoved it back in my face; they turned and left.

I was shaking and slumped back against the low rock. I began to look at other soldiers which had come into view now and were surveying the area with binoculars in search of something or someone. It was time to leave, I thought as I rose, collected my gun and made my way slowly through the bush-covered hillside.

I was worried that the Germans would discover traces of the commandos, but mostly I feared that they would catch Greeks and beat them up until they would tell on us and admit that strangers were in the area.

I continued, and found a stream where at long last I could give a long refreshing drink of water to my parched throat. I sat down on some fallen tree branches to watch for Germans who would be searching the area. I was not out in the open, but I was not completely hidden either. To a passerby it would look as if I was just taking a relaxing rest.

After about ten minutes I heard noises which then stopped. I got up but couldn't see anyone. I started to move quickly away from the direction from which I heard the noises. After about five hundred metres I saw them and my heart leapt - Germans.

There were dozens of them spread across the hillside, moving like machines. Wherever I looked there were more. The mountain would not protect me now, I thought. The only choice, it seemed, was to head downward into the valley. This way I would not be so visible. The valley was long as I passed Valiliki and Loukia then crossed the Mesara valley. Once across it, I was in my own territory. I breathed easier and spontaneously made the sign of the cross.

My village eventually came into sight as I took the stony path which climbed towards my house - home sweet home. I was impatient. What would I see? I wanted to surprise my family. I wanted to jump through the windows calling out their names and leap into their arms.

Suddenly, my family and relatives appeared at the curve of the road waiting for me. They had been watching, expectantly. They ran towards me, hands outstretched, their eyes twinkling with delight and we embraced. They held me as if I were a bird ready to take a flight and escape. I was told that everyone thought I had been killed in action.

The wife of my friend Badouvas also greeted me. You remember that we parted at Aghios Nicholas because the heat had exhausted him. When I asked her where he was she began to scream and viciously pull at her hair as if she wanted to tear it from her head.

"He should have been with you. What happened?" she cried bitterly.

I explained where I had left him and that he would be safe from German patrols and that she should not worry. Then I decided to go in search of him. I went to village Pyrgos, where I entered a coffee house. People were gathered in groups at the corners of the room. The deserted tables had on them half-empty cups of coffee. Others sat with heads bowed or looking suspiciously as if hiding dreadful secrets about the imminent danger of death. I listened momentarily. There was hopeless talk about we rebels doing a bad job and Germans were blockading the valleys. The people were whispering words of death. I ordered coffee but didn't drink much of it because my mind began to whirl. I'm in a village where the fear of Germans has taken control. 'Run for your life Basil,' I thought.

Panagia was my next stop. There was an atmosphere of panic there too, but fortunately I met someone I knew, Yiannis Agrimakis, who told me that Badouvas had been captured but later escaped.

With that news I headed home to see if he had made it and was overjoyed to discover that he had arrived while I was away.

After a short time we left together for the mountains.

## THE FORMING OF THE 'GESTAPITES' SECURITY FORCE

After the slaughter of Vianno and the burning of Rodakino, while we were trying to give courage to the local people, and lift their spirits, some Greek collaborators, or 'Germanofili', took advantage of people's panic and formed a security force like the German Gestapo and they acted like the Gestapo; that's why we called them Gestapites. Before the slaughter, they didn't have the nerve to make any such move because we, the rebels, would scare them off. We would raid their houses at night, where we would threaten them. But after what happened in Vianno and Rodakino, the Gestapites saw that the people were now more afraid, even terrified, thus becoming easy prey.

The Gestapites took the opportunity to get themselves organized and formed a force with a German, named Subert, as their leader. They went to the villages and terrorized people, brutalized them, stole from them, did everything they pleased. We were helpless to prevent them because we were afraid of German reprisals. The Gestapites were less than five per cent of the whole Cretan population, the rest of the population was against the German occupation and supported the resistance in many valuable ways. During the time when the Gestapites were active, we felt helpless, and tried to avoid any clashes with them, or the Germans -- Crete is just an island, a limited space – our movements were very restricted. We were not on the offensive, but we would undertake whatever sabotage we were told by the allied headquarters. The outcome of all this was that we, the rebels, were in a tough position.

The Gestapites not only ruined and terrified people, but also tried to recruit people to inform on us, threatening them with death if they didn't. There was a man who killed his father during a disagreement over family property and the distribution of it. He approached us, wanting to join our forces, but I turned him down because it would have given us a bad image. You see, we represented ourselves as liberators and defenders of high patriotic ideas, and we didn't want to tarnish our image by associating ourselves with a murderer.

When the authorities captured him and were about to punish him for his crime, the Gestapites seized the opportunity to recruit him. They told him that if he joined them, his life would be spared, and so he became a Gestapite. He was the worst kind of Gestapite – we didn't even want to mention his name. We just called him that 'Gestapite'. A lot of people were so afraid of him that they offered him whatever goods they could spare, and his family became one of the richest in Crete. Also the rest of the Gestapites lived well by the goods the people sent to appease them.

We tried to find a way to get rid of him, but it wasn't easy because we were afraid of the Germans. After hearing that some people, seeing that this man was living so well, thought that they would be better off by becoming Gestapites, I made up my mind to eliminate him. The English and city officials were against any effort to stop the Gestapites, for fear of German reprisals, but I was adamant and took a dictatorial approach, insisting that we do something about them.

One day my friends, the English, and I, were at the house of the president of our community, and we talked about how we could stop the Gestapites. We came up with two possibilities: either we could bribe their leader, Subert or we could send a couple of our own people to enlist as Gestapites, who would then set bombs in the German camp while the Gestapites were standing in line to get food.

While we were discussing these things, a fellow rebel came in with a letter for me. It was written by that Gestapite murderer, saying he wanted to see me in the village Demati, to talk to me about something. After reading the letter I told my friends that I would go to see him the next day. I would tell him that he was a criminal, and that even though I wanted to save him, I could not because of his crimes. I would find an opportunity to plant a bomb and leave.

My friends objected to the plan, saying that I might be killed and that I should not go ahead with it. But I insisted that I would go and just tell him the truth, that we were planning to kill him and he had better stop his criminal actions.

I left the next day with a man named George Filraki. On our way we passed through a village named Filipon. In the deserted street, one could hear only the sound of women mourning, the men had disappeared. I asked what had happened, and the people told me that the man I was going to meet had come into their village and had beaten, and burned several people. In fact, at one point, in a place called Kaliska, he burned several women by putting them in the outdoor hot ovens. He unashamedly bragged about it to me later; even his leader Subert disapproved of it.

After this, I didn't want to meet him, as anyone seeing me with him might very easily say: "The Gestapites come and terrorize us, and yet you rebels are in league with them."

The Gestapite murderer had six or seven others cooperating with him. One time four of them went to another village, named Ini, close to my village, where they terrorized people. The president of one community, a patriot, knew the German governor of that section of the island. The president told the governor about their deeds and asked him to intervene. He actually sent a detachment of soldiers to arrest the four Gestapites and took them to the village Kefalohori, where they were beaten and then sent in chains to jail in the city of Heraklion.

Soon after the Gestapites were imprisoned, I sent a message: "You see what happened to your friends? The same will happen to you. The Germans are not to be trusted. It's about time for you to leave the Germans and come with us, or go to the English."

We were trying to make him desert the Germans of his own free-will. That way he would tell his family and relatives that he was not a Gestapite any more and his family would not inform on us rebels. No matter how we tried he would not desert – he seemed to have no conscience – although he gave us the idea that he was considering our idea.

When we learned that the Germans went to his house at night to meet with him, I decided to confront him myself. As I approached his house I noticed smoke coming out of its chimney and I thought to myself: 'How about that, the traitor is warm and cozy.'

After greeting him I said, "The Germans will do to you what they did to your friends. Now is the time to come with us because I've heard that you were thinking about it."

I watched him carefully. He was sitting by his fireplace, and by the way he sat, he gave an impression of contentment. I couldn't help thinking: 'be warm and comfortable tonight, my friend, but tomorrow be gone.'

"I heard that you're thinking of coming to our side," I said.

He smiled sardonically, showing his bad teeth, as he said, "My friend, don't believe what you hear. My position with the Germans was never so secure as it is now. The Germans were here the last two nights to confer with me."

Seeing that he lacked any conception of morality I felt disgust, but I didn't show it. I just said, "Okay, if you think that you are secure with the Germans, it's okay with me."

Then I left for my base. I realized then, that he had to be eradicated no matter what the cost. Either way, dead or alive, the Gestapite man would be the cause of death and destruction.

We held a conference and made a plan. We decided to kidnap him, and do it in such a way that it would look like a defection. Following that plan, we sent one of our members dressed as a deputy, along with another person, to tell the Gestapite murderer that his boss Subert wanted to see him, and that he should go with them, which he did. We told the villagers that when the Germans asked about the Gestapite murderer, they should say that he had left on his own, obviously on his own free-will, but that they didn't know where. We forced his wife to testify that her husband had probably defected. She was told that if she didn't do this, he would die.

The Germans just made a simple investigation; there were no retaliations as we had feared. They didn't care about the fate of Greek traitors, only their own. At last the communities breathed free of the terror of that Gestapite murderer.

There was another Gestapite called Emilio who used to beat people up. Once a friend of mine came across Emilio who hit him mercilessly, using the stick that my friend carried. But unknown to him, the stick, that my friend was transporting, held secret notes and papers in a hollow. My friend told me that, "all the time he was hitting me I wasn't so concerned about the beating as I was that the stick would break and Emilio would find the secret papers. I even moved in such a way to reduce the force of the blows and protect the stick."

After the war ended, we learned that Emilio, had been an agent for English intelligence, and in order to be convincing in his role, he would only hit people.

After the elimination of the Gestapite murderer, I didn't go back to the Lasiotika Mountains. Those mountains were unsuitable to me after the ruin of Vianno and after the splintering of the rebel forces into rightist and leftist factions. My areas of action from then on would be farther south: Tsoutsouro, Housakas and the Asteroussia Mountains.

Some time passed and things went on routinely. Tom Dobadin and my friend Souris left on a mission to the Middle East for a while. In the meantime, in Ierapetra, a southern port of Crete, some Greek commandos landed - Temouralkis, Agelousis, and others. Tired, and on the lookout for Germans, they wandered along the coast trying to find a good place to hide. On their way they were picked up by a German patrol who questioned them, but in the end the Germans let them go and kept only their donkey. Probably the donkey looked more suspicious to them! I wasn't involved in their mission because in essence I should not even know they existed.

There were different kinds of intelligence operations. One intelligence group was not supposed to know anything about the operations of other groups, but these people could not go anywhere, and they came to our place for help.

Those commandos had come to gather information for a report about German planes sitting on the Kastelli airfield, and also to gather information about German movements as a preliminary to the abduction of the German general, Kreiper. Whenever the allied forces were to carry out an operation on German airfields, they would send commandos beforehand to gather information on German movements. Our mission was, as in this case, to protect, guide and help the commandos when they needed our help.

It was February, 1944, a period of increased resistance activity. We were bolder toward the Germans. Tom Dobadin sent a message for me to go and see him in a place named Amari. When I went there to see Tom, I told him again about wanting to change the place where we were conducting our missions from the village, Archedria to another village, Demati.

The reason for the change was that the Archedria area was very rough with steep cliffs making it hard for the animals to go through the area carrying the heavy loads of weapons and explosives that we were receiving from the Middle East, and Demati was situated better.

Although I had decided on the change, I had to get approval from the English. At Amari, I told Tom about my decision.

He looked at a map and said, "I told you there are sheep-breeders around that area and as they're going to see our movements, they might betray us."

"How could those shepherds be traitors if the Germans have already killed some of their relatives?"

"I don't know, Basil, I just have doubts."

"You shouldn't," I said.

"Okay, go ahead as you said... but the area might be dangerous, the Germans might have put land mines there," Tom replied.

"If the area had been mined, I would have known. I'm always informed from my people, but to make sure, I will go there, to test the area myself."

"That sounds fine, Basil".

After testing the area with some animals to see if anything happened, I asked the shepherds if they had detected anything unusual.

They said, "We would have told you if we had," and added, "In order to have freedom of movement why don't you get a permit from the Germans to use the area for breeding animals as we do."

"Why would the Germans do a favor for us... after all they're not... our Koumbari," I said with a laugh.

"You know, there are other ways, Basil. Why won't you plead with them... flatter them... give them presents. It never fails. Do what we do anytime we need a permit," they said.

The area was perfect for our missions because we could get from our base to the coast in one day, whereas from Archedria, we would need two to three days. It was possible to make our arrangements during the day and be at the beach that night. Then we would give the signals for the boat to approach, unload the ship, load the donkeys or mules, and be back at our base, all in the same night.

Then we settled in our new base.

## AFTER THE ABDUCTION OF KREIPER

The abduction of the German general, Kreiper, for a show of strength, by the allied forces in charge of a military division in Crete, was a cause for more retaliations against the Cretan people. The Germans threatened to inflict punishment on the Cretans if Kreiper wasn't returned to them, which they did, by destroying the villages of Anogia and Amari.

The morning after the abduction, a person named Farmakis came to notify me that Germans were surrounding his village towards the area where we had arranged with the allied forces to drop supplies by parachute at night, but it was too late to change plans now. We were to set fires for signals towards north, west and east of the dropping point. This way we could get them fast and then disappear into the darkness.

As we were readying ourselves, one of the locals came to tell us that the Germans were too close. I thought the operation had been betrayed. I told him to go back and watch their movements and to keep us informed.

We discovered that the Germans had taken hold of the surrounding mountains and were moving fast towards the dropping area. We dispersed in every direction for cover. The Germans combed the area in a ten to fifteen kilometre area, covering all the hills, shooting at the grass and up into trees.

I could see, through binoculars, the glare from the lights of a German car and closer I saw my cousin signaling me to go towards him. I was aware of the danger of my position. If the Germans went across the hill from where I was they would have seen me. I was on a bare plain. There were only a few large rocks and some widely dispersed bushes and shrubs in my area. I had no refuge and was visible to anyone on the mountain side. I looked around. I couldn't hide anywhere. There seemed to be no way out of my predicament.

Then I looked down on Earth. Yes! 'Mother Earth with her dents and crevices could be the answer to my prayers,' I thought. There! I ran forward and almost dived into a deep crevice and folded myself into a crouching position, trying to become invisible. There I stayed for a while, hearing only the sounds of grenades fading into the distance as if drawn into space, moving farther and farther away.

I decided it was safe for me to get out and go towards the mountains. I knew the area very well and I wasn't afraid. I figured the Germans had already captured the shepherds in the area and were probably moving further away. The minute I started up the hill I saw my brother-in-law and a young boy named Alanis Sfougarakis running. I called to them to wait, so we could run together down the hill towards the grazing grounds where the Germans would be holding any shepherds as prisoners.

We were within the enemy's range, almost at the tip of their guns and what saved us was that we saw the donkeys. They were tied to some rocks. "Donkeys... donkeys," said the young boy.

"Germans! Germans!" I said, "There are Germans around."

"Where? Where?" the boy said, "I don't see any Germans."

"Come on! The Germans are the donkeys and the donkeys are the Germans.

"Why?"

"Because Greeks wouldn't be here with donkeys as we are in a dead zone. That means Germans are here."

"The Germans are not only rams as in our signal, but donkeys too, now, Uncle Basil!" said the boy with a wide grin discovering a new idea.

We turned sharply around and off we went. I parted from my companions for if we were caught, they might under German threats, reveal my true identity. I checked to make sure that my phony identification card was with me.

From sparse undergrowth, I gazed through thorny bushes at German figures moving along brushing the area. The day was clear. I was visible from every side, and it seemed that there was no place to hide. I felt abandoned in a bare hostile land where everybody was against me. Looking in every direction, I could see Germans everywhere, even the rocks seemed like German figures to me.

I ran north, and eventually found a place where water disappeared into a hole in the ground giving me the idea that the ground would be my protector once again. Crawling into a shallow depression, I tried to make myself flat with the ground and I pulled some branches over me for cover. There I was, lying motionless like a rabbit... not daring to move and thinking that maybe I should take a peak to see what was going on, when a voice directly above me called something in German.

I froze.

Through the branch leaves which covered me, I could just make out a dusty black boot and the grey of uniform trousers. The boots kicked my branches and I felt like I wanted to pull the legs.

'Here I got you... this time I can get you by the legs, not by the gun,' I thought daringly, but I let my breath out slowly so as not to make any noise.

Were they moving away? Gun shots retorted loudly and still very close by. The knot in my stomach returned and I pulled my legs and held in tighter, pressing myself down into the hard earth. Silence - there was silence. They must have gone, I thought. I lifted my head... I must look. I lifted the branches and peaked out.

The flash of explosions blinded me momentarily as the universe itself seemed to reverberate at the power of the shock wavers. The lights of the Germans' cars were not visible any more. The Germans had apparently gone past my area.

I got up and ran and ran until I saw a figure ahead of me in the distance, also moving quickly through a quiet empty field. He was a friend of mine. He turned and his face lit up as he saw me.

"Hey Basil, you know those bloody Germans shot at me, but they missed. I was too far away."

"They missed me too, but I was under their feet," I quipped.

We both laughed and kept running for our lives.

Just after the abduction of Kreiper we carried out a sabotage mission of blowing up some German vehicles near a village named Damasta. But the Germans retaliated and killed ten to twenty people. Shortly after the killings, a German commander named Syfis sent an order to the village of Anogia that about fifty men from the village must begin compulsory work in the fields.

Syfis was angry because weapons had been found in Anogia after he had been told by the villagers that there were none. The men of Anogia refused to join a work gang, so a number of Gestapites and Italian Nazis, went to the village to get them by force. They were too late; the men had left Anogia and gone into hiding.

Feeling cheated, the Germans decided to get even with them. They did not burn the village or go on a rampage, – anything like that – but guess what... they kidnapped the village women and march out of the village.

However, the Germans didn't realize that by doing this they would touch a soft spot in the Greek nature 'philotimo' (pride). The men, feeling ashamed to be in hiding when the Germans had their women, quickly gathered together outside the village and made plans to trap the Germans...

And that's how it was.

The men hid outside the village, set a trap, encircled the Germans and ambushed them to free the women, then imprisoned Syfis and his companions.

## The Burning of Anogia

The burning of the village Anogia in retaliation for the abduction of Kreiper was a tragedy. My wife lived in that village before we met. She told me how she and members of her family escaped and what the Germans did there. This is her account:

"My father, who was both the village priest and teacher, was taking a nap when he heard a voice saying, "Father, get up. This is no time to sleep."

He rose and went outside. Passing the church, he left the village, listening as if he knew that he would hear something. And he did. When outside of the village he heard the signal: "Rams...rams... the rams are in the vineyards!"

This time there were about fourteen thousand Germans surrounding our village of three thousand people. My father went back to the village and rang the church bell and other church bells followed. Hearing the bells people began to flee the village for Psyloriti mountain to hide.

Only those who could run fast made it. Parents who could not find all their children had to leave them behind. Sick and old people were left behind. The first houses were quickly set alight and those within or on the streets were shot or blown apart by grenades. The Germans shot randomly at people – old or young, anyone, anywhere. The old and sick who were confined in their houses were the first to die.

My house was by the church and my father came back as fast as he could to tell us to leave right away. I only had time to put my sandals on and with my father, one of my sisters, and with some relatives and neighbours ran to the mountain. My brother and younger sister were left behind.

We went deep into a mountain cave where there were already about one hundred people. We stayed there in the darkness, silent until somebody said, "I can't stand it any more, I'll suffocate in here" and he started to leave.

My father stopped him saying, "Where are you going? You're going to betray us. Germans are all around us, and they'll drop a bomb outside here and kill us all if they see you."

In the morning we all left the cave and headed in different directions. My father, my sister, myself and about twenty others headed farther up into the mountains where we met another group of people from our village and a group of the underground forces. From there we could see the devastation the Germans were reaping upon my village.

The destruction continued the whole time they had the village under blockade, for days. Those houses that were spared the first assault were emptied of whatever worthwhile things they contained, such as food and clothes. All other things were smashed and the dwellings set on fire. With the continued fires and bombing of village the underground group told us all to leave because they were going to fight the Germans and try to push them out of our village.

We separated into small groups heading in different directions. We all chose different routes as if we were choosing the best path for survival, the best way to beat the odds. We went on without food or water. The sandals that were my only protection against the rough earth, as we walk and walk for miles in our struggle for life, started to brake, and I dragged them as I went along trying to keep up. Keep up, keep up, I kept saying to myself, trying to find the courage to go on.

We passed a couple of villages and our group split again. Reaching another, my father asked us if we wanted to stay there or go on. The choice was ours. We decided to go on, but my father decided to stay there for the time being. Now almost everyone in my family had scattered in different directions. The group of refugees I was with passed the village Idrito. Here the Germans had just killed twenty-five people. Afraid that we might be spotted and shot, we decided to go on. We walked along dusty, desolate roads. My sandals tore a little more with each step and I kept dragging them. The land around us looked barren and devoid of any living creature. Hunger and thirst tormented us all.

Suddenly a human figure silhouetted against the sky. We thought we saw a vision, a young girl holding a pita bread, but it wasn't an illusion, she was real. She came closer and we crowded around her, asking for a mouthful each to curb our hunger. She gave us the bread and we divided it between the twenty-four of us, a small bite for each of us. We continued our long trek until we reached a village where somebody offered us shelter for the night.

In the morning a neighbor told us we weren't safe there because the Germans had threatened them with reprisals if they shelter any refugees. We went on and reached the village of Gergeri where the people gave us food but told us that they could not take care of us because they were afraid of German reprisals. There, a woman I knew, told me that she had heard that the Germans had killed my brother in a village close to Anogia. She said my brother was among those shot outside the church. Upon hearing the news my sister and I wanted to return to Anogia.

However, we continued a little way, but since we could not find any food or shelter, our group split up again and some of us reluctantly returned to Gergeri. There we were lucky to hide in a house for nineteen days.

After that time our group decided to go back to Anogia. On our way back, we passed through other villages where we were told that my brother was alive and that some people thought they had seen him somewhere. In the same way we continued on getting food and staying some nights in different villages. We dragged on our odyssey feeling half-way alive and half-way dead.

With my sandals completely falling apart now, dragging them just for enough cover over sharp stones or rocks, we passed about fourteen villages until eventually coming close to Anogia, where we stopped at a place named Katharo. There we found other people from my village, camping out and hiding. They would go to our village undercover of darkness to salvage anything the Germans might have left behind. We did the same.

My house had been burned and was leveled to the ground. Near it lay a dead woman covered with thousands of crawling and dancing flies. Everywhere dead people and dead animals lay where they dropped. The village stank of rotting flesh.

In my aunt's house we found only some books which we took. They were the only things we ever recovered. Everything else was lost.

Thirty-five days later, our family was united. Luckily, we all survived. My brother escaped safely, but my younger sister found herself in a blockade when she was picking oranges from the trees. When she saw the approaching Germans, she didn't panic, but in her youth's innocence which made her immune to danger, she continued to pick up oranges. Undisturbed she kept on picking oranges, glancing at the Germans as if to say, "Don't you have anything better to do today?" and the Germans just passed on.

## Running for Death

Before the Germans burned my wife's village Anogia, they blocked my village too, either to catch any underground activity they were suspicious of or to intimidate us from supporting the resistance.

The Germans searched from house to house, taking prisoners and lining them up in the school yard. Those who heard the signal, warning of coming Germans, hid if they had time. We used our attic to hide.

The Germans kicked and broke the doors of our house. They looked everywhere, underneath beds and inside closets. We stayed motionless until they left... until we heard a long, shrill desperate cry which curdled our blood... not from far away.

As the Germans rounded up people, they saw through their binoculars a man, a captain and a local administrator, who had some document papers on him, heading towards the mountain. They pursued him and caught him. As they returned to the village, the man, even with his hands tied, escaped.

He ran for life, with strength and courage, jumping over crevices, weaving to the shots, slipping off the bullets of death as he tried to get out of shooting range. The eyes of all in the school yard followed him with reverence, watching the impossible, to miraculously evade the vicious gunshots raining around him.

Although the odds were against that man, he was making a clear getaway, until... his run was for death now, for he lost his balance and fell, becoming an easy target... outrageous... horribly unfair.

With the last shot, the prisoners' shrill sorrowful unison cry pierced our attic walls. Shaken-up and forgetting anything else, we climbed up on the roof of our house to see what was happening.

From our vantage point we saw in the school yard the rounded up people... some of them spotted us and waved desperately for us to get out of sight and hide. We did.

Later, the people went and picked up the body of that man and buried him. After the war a statue was erected for his courageous act.

## FUNNY AND PECULIAR INCIDENTS DURING THE RESISTANCE

These stories indicate that perhaps war is not what we think it is, the enemy, the weapons, the premeditated strategic plans, the superior military might, that can overcome everything. Perhaps war is the uncontrollable human factor reaching forwards creating states of shock, states of misery, states of rapture: states of the impossible and the outrageous.

### The Beggars

My house in the village was primitive compare to today's houses. It was comprised of a big room downstairs which was the living room, and a couple of rooms upstairs. Next to the living room was the stable with our animals, some donkeys and some cows. The living room had a wooden floor made from logs, instead of bare ground as was usual in other houses. As the stable was separate, my house was considered to be one of the most luxurious in the village.

At one time, when I came down to my house, I found the door locked and none of my family around. I knew my mother would have left the key, as always, under an old piece of wood by the old door. I got what I needed and since no one was in the house, I didn't want to stay. I was ready to leave when a friend of mine, a collaborator in the resistance came to talk to me about getting some people on the caique for the Middle East. Among these people was a distant uncle of mine, a respected person whose sons, a lawyer and a doctor, had been persecuted by the Germans. His sons had already gone ahead to the Middle East. For no other reason I would have gone back to the house. Once we sat down, I heard a voice calling me from outside, "Basil... Basil..."

I looked out of a small window set in one of the thick walls of my house. It was one of my aunts, who lived nearby, calling me. She came running and said, "Basil, Basil, close the door! Germans are coming."

I asked what kind of Germans did she mean: the regular troops or the ones whom we called beggars. The beggars were the ones who would go at random, on their own, day or night, from village to village, asking for different things like eggs, cheeses, or bread. Of course, a lot of times they would ask what they wanted, but a lot of times they would steal. It was important that we stay in good terms with them, so as not to arouse their suspicions. When they came to our houses we would offer them drinks like the one we make,'raki' and other goodies like raisins, and nuts.

Sometimes their visits would create absurd situations in the course of our operations of coming and going through a village to arrange things, as when English officers were with us, and the beggars appeared.

They would often stay until dinner. Probably they loved our food or our... hospitality, or simply they didn't like the food at their camp, I don't know! We would be in one house eating and drinking with the beggars, and right next door we with our English friends, would be eating and drinking... to health, to good-luck, and to... hide and seek... so much that the English would make wisecracks about our comings and goings between the houses in checking the action!

"Eh! How you treat your royal visitors tonight? Do you serve them drinks on the rocks? Or they stay with your raki?"

Or sometimes regular German troops would pass by while the beggars were eating and drinking with us. Then, the English would ask jokingly, "What's your signal to warn the enemy about the enemy, Basil?"

One time I had a gun with me, and I had to hide it from the beggars who were fast approaching my doorstep. 'Where would I put it?' I wondered. Looking around to find a good place to hide my gun, my eyes glanced at some shelves by the door where my mother had put some yarn and the idea came to me to hide the gun in the yarn. Feeling sure that it would be amongst things unneeded by the beggars I hid it there. Meanwhile, my aunt stood at the door telling the Germans in Greek that nobody was inside, but they didn't understand her and pushed their way into the house. As soon as they came in, they went straight towards the yarn. At that critical moment, I jumped in front of the yarn, saying in broken German, "No, madam's house these! No! No!" And I almost pushed them to make them look somewhere else. I directed their attention to a bottle of our homemade liqueur and I told them to have a drink first. They liked that idea.

I breathed.

For the time being I had stopped them from getting the yarn. They sat down. Remembering that one of the English had called them "royal highnesses" I thought, 'Let's put the drinks on a tray and serve them with class. Seeing the drinks like that they might stay for more drinking and forget the yarn.'

I served them again... They got up again and headed towards the yarn.

"Do you want another drink?"

"Ya! Ya!" they said.

And the scene was repeated, they would have a drink, then head for the yarn, then another drink.

'My gosh,' I thought. 'This is more than just hide and seek. It's come and get it... they're getting me this time all right... what a shame, they're getting me for just some yarn!'

The pressure was tremendous. There seemed to be no way out. 'Where are your resources to find a way out, Basil?' I thought to myself again, as I carried them another tray of drinks. But each time as I was figuring out how to get them to lose interest in the yarn, my agony grew making my hands shake so much that the glasses tipped while filling them, while carrying them as to hit each other making a noise, 'dan, dan, dan.'

'That can become my resource, Basil,' I thought, 'to use my shaking condition to my advantage.' I made funny steps. "Oh, oh," I would say, stepping wildly, like dancing trying to go with the motion of the glasses, to balance the glasses.'Ah, ah', I was saying, while stepping backwards, forward and sideways, with movements of my back to the yarn and my hands to shake non-stop.

'You're a star Basil,' I said to myself, trying to keep on, to keep the outrageous. I sang and danced under the shadows of their guns, one, two, three, with my feet in every direction and my back on one, to cover the view to the yarn.

Then all of a sudden they looked at me curiously as they discovered something: I was retarded.

"What's your name?" they said with strange smiles.

"Don't know... name?" I replied making a gesture and pointing to the door, blinking my eyes, and saying at the same time, "Aaa! Aaa!" and the Germans, "Ha , ha" laughing the whole time.

Another drink and they were gone. My performance was enough.

They took yarn from another house later.

The question, why they wanted the yarn? bothered us until we found the answer. They wanted it to send it back home.

## The Monk's Hole

When the commandos for the abduction of Kreiper came, I sent them for safety to a monastery. I sent them there because I knew the head monk, who had offered me his monastery as a refuge before. Actually, to put it in his words, the monk had said to me, "Whenever you need a place to hide from the Germans, I have the safest place in my monastery. It's in a place you won't expect. It's used to be a fermentation hole and it's small and handy. That's why I'm not afraid of the Germans, if they ever come after me. I'm not afraid because I got my secret hideaway. I got my secret hole!"

The commandos came back safe and sound.

"Eh! how was your stay?" I asked them noticing their crumpled clothes, their dishevelled appearance... and their smell.

They smelled musty.

"I'll tell you my friend, we'll never forget the place."

"Probably because it's a monastery," I said.

"Not because of its holiness, but of its horrors."

I looked at them with surprise.

"See what happened," they said, "We were in the dining room of the monastery, sitting around a big rough table, having dinner when there was knock on the door. A monk looked through the hole in the door, and he came back to tell us that there were Germans looking for food. We jumped up asking where we could hide. At that the monk bent down under the table and signaled for us to follow him. "Oh, no, what is he doing, is he going nuts?" We asked one another. "Hide us under the table?" But then we saw him pulling two boards from the wooden floor, which revealed a hole. "Oh, no," we said again, "not for us."

"Come on," he said, pointing to it.

"We won't fit through that," we said.

"Yes, you will," and he almost shoved us into the hole.

And there we were sinking down to depths of darkness such as the darkness of hell.

"Come on you guys, don't exaggerate over little time in a hole.

It couldn't have been so bad. I have been in holes like that. What's the difference?"

"Nothing would make us go in there again, we don't want to die there like cowards trapped like rats, without ever having the chance to fight back. Anywhere but there," they said in agreement.

"Big deal," I said grinning.

"My God, it's not the kind of death we deserved. We didn't come so far to die like rats in a hole."

"What can I say Basil!" a Commando said, "It was awful. It was pitch black. You couldn't see your hand in front of your face. There was no light at all. When the abbot replaced the floor boards it was black - as hell! And the smell!" He wrinkled his nose. "I can smell it," he said, with disgust. "And of course we had to stay as quiet as church... while the Germans ate lunch over our heads!"

Some time later, with some friends of mine, I had to go to see a Greek general who had come from Egypt, and he was staying there for safety. It was a warm day. We had the window open. We were sitting around the table, eating and resting comfortably with our feet stretched out while we talked, but the monk kept looking out of the open window.

"Hey," I said to him, "why do you keep looking outside? Do you think the Germans will come back for food this time again? Are they going to be hungry at the same time again? Come on, relax," I said to him remembering the commandos.

"Just to make sure," he said, shooting a sober glance at me, scarcely noticing what I was saying, and he just kept on looking out the window. We continued talking when the monk suddenly jumped up. "Germans!" he said, "Quickly... come on! Into the hole."

We looked at him, in surprise. It couldn't be. But there we were going into the hole, first the general and then ourselves, falling down into the darkness, to the depths of hell. The floor boards were replaced. All of a sudden time stood still, eternity surrounded us and darkness engulfed us, as we were like sardines packed in a sealed tin, and what a pungent smell! It was suffocating, yes, suffocating and slowly paralysing. 'Is this hell?' I thought. "I can't survive anymore," I said in desperation and tried to get out, but my friends held me. I was ready to explode - to bang on the ceiling, to push my way out.

"Come on, Basil, do you want to get us killed?"

We crouched in silence for a little awhile. Then, blessed relief, there was light. And then the abbot's face. "You can come out now," he said. "You were lucky," he continued, "you didn't have to stay in there very long."

I looked at him in disbelief. "Lucky?" I said.

"Yes, those weren't Germans but Greeks in German shirts. I was just playing it safe."

**Going For Snails**

It was a hot day. An English officer and I were travelling across country on a mission until we had to pass the village of Amari, a rugged village up on a mountain slope. We didn't know anybody there. The English officer was dressed like us, the country locals, and as he was tanned from travelling we were sure he wouldn't be recognized even to his closest friends. We approached the village and noticed the public water fountain where people were getting water. There were women collecting drinking water, and men filling up containers to give to their horses. We were tired and thirsty.

There was nothing better than getting a drink of water from that fountain where the water, like in a stream, ran fast, refreshing and cool. The spray cooled the air around. Sure that the English wouldn't be recognized we approached and mingled with the crowd. We weren't. We were standing waiting for our turn when I felt I was being stared at; you know the feeling of somebody's eyes heavy on you. I looked around and saw a tall typical Cretan man, watching both of us as if he was inspecting us.

"Your companion is English, isn't he?" He said to me as he was approaching us.

"No, he isn't," I said defensively.

"Yes, he is," he insisted. "He doesn't look like a Greek, and... since he is a visitor I would like both of you to come to my house as guests for dinner."

"I looked at him trying to find out what was behind the open smiling face, with fiery dark Cretan eyes. Was he a friend, or was he pretending to be a friend? Was he sincere or did he have an ulterior motive? My instinct said that he looked too Cretan to be otherwise. Should we trust to appearances? Or, does our instinct follow reasons? Then, I should make the right conversation that would have drawn the right answers proving or disapproving if he was a patriot. And he was.

"We're glad to accept your invitation," I told him at last.

With eyes showing delight, he then said, "Follow me to my humble house." It was a two-story house with beds of flowers and shrubs in its yard.

From that time we became friends, and whether I and my companions had to go though that village, we stayed in his house, but only in the daytime when we would be easily notified of oncoming Germans. The night we would spend sleeping outside the house in order to be on alert for Germans.

One such time, we went through that village and we stopped at the house of our friend again. He had prepared a beautiful Cretan dinner with all the trimmings, as our cheeses and our raki.

We were enjoying our eating and drinking so much that we didn't notice the bad weather outside, but Aristidis did as he said, "You're not going to spend the night outside. It's such bad weather that you're going to get sick and I don't want you to leave sick from my house."

"We have to, for there are Germans around," I said.

"Listen, as far as I know there are no Germans around, at least for tonight," he said.

He kept on like that and since he was confident about it he persuaded us to stay in.

We were sound asleep in the early hours of the following morning when we heard banging on the door. We jumped up.

"Germans!" we said. "Where can we go? Where can we hide? We must find a way to get away from the house," we said to each other.

"Wait, don't talk," Aristidis said, and keeping calm he went to the door and said, "Who is it?"

There was no answer.

Meanwhile I and my companions looked around carefully to find a way out of the house. We were on the second floor and the windows were the only way out. There wasn't any other solution than to climb out of the windows.

"At least we would land on a beautiful flowerbed," I said.

"Maybe we can land on our beautiful... deathbed," Panos, our comrade remarked.

"Don't you want a beautiful deathbed? At least we'll be surrounded by beauty, not by ugly bullets," I said, jokingly. "Maybe the flowers and bushes would be like a springboard supporting us as we would be bouncing and jumping..."

"Like in a circus," my comrade interrupted me.

"But we are already in a circus," I said.

"What circus?" he said.

"In a circus of war, and..."

A loud knocking interrupted us again.

We stood still. There were more knocks, again more silence, again no answer.

"Hey! You guys, there is not time for jokes anymore. Let's get to it," I finally said.

Panos climbed up to the window, stepping on the carved bureau that was set under it. At this intense moments Aristidis said, "I don't think it's Germans. When they knock they call out or break down the door."

His explanation made sense – at least for me, and we stopped climbing.

"No, don't open the door! It's a gamble... Maybe it's a trick," Panos said, his feet hanging from the bureau.

"I think," Aristidis stated, "my instincts tell me that whoever is outside is not a German. I can tell from the kind of knocking."

"Your instincts! Why should I trust them?" Panos said.

"Because I have good reasons to follow my instinct," Aristidis responded firmly.

"And instincts are based on good reasons, at least sometimes," I couldn't help saying.

"Look," Aristidis said, "I'll go downstairs, I'll open the door a crack and have a peak of who is outside. If there is danger I'll whistle. You'll have time to escape or are you in such a hurry to fly through the window?"

"Yes, come on, that's reasonable," I said.

"Okay," Panos nodded. "I wait and I'll stay up there." He remained on the bureau.

Aristidis crept downstairs. We all waited. He opened the door a crack. With pail in hand there he stood, a deaf boy, friend of Aristidis' son.

Aristidis returned quickly. He looked at Panos on the bureau.

"'Poulaki mou' (my kid). It was a deaf boy who wanted to collect snails out in the fields, with my son."

Everyone laughed and pointed at Panos.

## Digging For Salt

We were at the Lasiotika Mountains. At one time, Leigh Fermor, came to us and told me that I had to find another spot for our rendezvous point, more safe, by the sea, that nobody would eventually know. We went at nightime to the sea under the shadows of the nearby German outposts and the surrounding countryside, close to the area of Tsoutsouro, to pick out the spot. We climbed down the precipitous mountain slopes along the coast, but it was so dark that we could not use a flashlight for fear we would be visible to the two Germans outposts that were close by. This way we didn't finish what we set out to do and headed home.

On our way back we saw people, who at that time of the year, in the summer, would go to the beaches at night and would collect water that had a high content of salt. For that, they would dig trenches where the sea water would settle. There, the water would condense in eight days and leave a residue of salt that later would be collected and sold.

That night we saw some people digging in trenches, but they could not see us in the dark. They heard us coming and fell face down on the sand, hoping that we would pass them. But we didn't pass them as they hoped because we were looking to find a right spot, and almost stepped on two of them.

Thinking that they were Germans, I pulled out my gun ready to shoot when I heard them, as they were scared to death, mumbling, "My God, my God!" Then I realized that they were Greeks. If I hadn't heard them saying, "My God," I would have shot them and then all of us would have been in danger because the nearby Germans would have heard the shots.

Talking about digging salt, there is another incident that involved one of our best guides, Manolio Bisberaki. He would usually be dressed in a German uniform, pretending to be a German when we were out on our missions, and we had to pass near people. This way we could get by without the local people noticing us and make a scene to draw the attention of the Germans.

At the salt digging time of the year, we had to go to the beach on a mission. Manolio proceeded ahead as usual, but he came at arms length with some people who were gathering salt there, bending as they were in their trenches.

Manolio then for a joke and to make the people unsuspicious of us, started to talk German and interrogated them. "Kommen... nicht... verstanden? Manolio shouted with threatening gestures... and the people bending as they were in their trenches begging for mercy... "You... good German!"

The rest of us were hiding watching the scene and laughing up to a point that I thought we would give ourselves away, so I had to shout in German, "Nichts Kaput." (Don't kill them) to put an end to this outrageous scene.

Then Manolio told them in an commanding manner to get lost, and they vanished. This way, anytime we encountered incidents like that and Manolio was with us he pretended to be German, and the people never learned that we used the area for our missions.

### The Boy With the Supper

It was late of one dark and cold day in November, 1943, when my friend Badouvoyiannis and I left to check on our grazing animals on the rough, black, almost barren winter slopes in southern Crete.

We set out for a shack that we shepherds had in the mountains and used for protection from the weather while watching our flocks. Before leaving, we asked a neighbourhood boy, named Stylianos Kalomiris, to bring us supper at a particular time. After checking our animals we took the road to the shack and waited for the boy.

The night was very cold and windy.We sat around a dilapidated rough wooden table which could hardly supported the old, rusty oil lamp that was on it. As the wind rattled the single flimsy door continuously, we felt cold and strange. We tried to secure the door closed wedging it shut. But still the wind searched out nooks and crannies through which to blow, and our lamp flickered wildly.

"Did you hear that?" my friend Badouvoyiannis said.

"No," I replied. "It's nothing. Just the voice of the wind."

"But the wind sounds strange," my friend said.

We sat straining to hear something through the whistle of the mounting wind. We heard voices. Listening, we tried to distinguish what kind of voices they were.

"They're foreign voices, not Greek. They sound like Germans," my friend said.

At that we swung a back window open and threw ourselves through it onto cutting and bruising ourselves on the ground as shots rang out hitting the shack door. Germans had arrived.

"What do they want with the old shack?" we asked ourselves. But we were gone, having crawled away from the house to a safe spot behind a rock that stood out from the hillside like a monument. 'I hope it wouldn't be my memorial stone', I thought. We waited in agony watching the track for the boy who was supposed to come.

"Come on, let's crawl a little bit farther down the road to see if the boy is coming, and warn him about the Germans," I said to my friend.

With our eyes staring at where the road met the horizon we crawled slowly forward, but no boy came into sight. Then we saw that the Germans had set up flares to light the area around us, and we were forced to change our position, but always within sight of the road.

We waited and waited... for an eternity, it seemed. The boy didn't show up and we figured that if the Germans had come to such an isolated place where we were near a ravine it meant that either somebody had betrayed us or that the Germans had blockaded the surrounding area.

The night was overloading us with weariness, tension and apprehension. Even the darkness of the night was threatening. Every inch we crept forward, every inch we covered, would bring us nearer the boy, or at least that's what we hoped. Every moan and groan of the wind, every rustle of leaf or crack of twig was a German voice. The hours dragged unmercifully.

"Let's crawl to a safer hideout to spend the night, and in the morning we can decide what to do," we said in agreement.

We moved deeper into a ravine where, on the edge grew some bushes to cover us and protect us from the Germans' view, and we would not be visible in the morning. We went deeper and deeper.

Looking upwards we felt that the edge of the ravine had taken a different outlook for us. I lay on my back and looked up at the sky. The edges of the ravine towered over our heads. I felt suddenly naked as though anyone standing on the edge looking down would be able to pick us out like flies in milk. Was this place safe? Or were the edges of the ravine the teeth of a trap. The night kept on unfolding with ifs, buts, and hows, filling us with so many doubts and insecurities that our need for sleep was driven away. It went on and on.

"What if the Germans have caught the boy and tortured him in order to make him tell on us? What if the boy could not stand it for long and told them everything in every detail like where we hide in a blockade, or like where we would usually hide in the mountains? we thought.

"Look up, I see some shadows of German figures bending over, looking into the ravine!" I said. "They're coming down... down... down..."

"Where? Where?" My friend said anxiously.

"Up there, up there," I said pointing upwards, straining my voice.

My friend moved up cautiously to be able to see better. He came back. "Basil, I don't see anything. Are you joking?"

"No, I think I'm hallucinating," I said wearily.

The faces of the invisible enemies in the night were taking a toll on us.

"What if we face a possible blockade in the morning? What if the Germans are waiting for the daylight to search for us..." Badouvoyiannis said.

"Like a hunter looking for his... prey," I said skeptically.

"How are we going to face a possible blockade in the morning, Basil?"

"I don't know. Maybe the unknown would bring us a solution," I said, "or at least make us think of a solution."

We went over and over until there was no sense, or until nothing made sense anymore.

The daylight found us drained, stuck in a crevice of the ravine's rocky ground.

"Basil, I think the thing for us is not to move until we hear voices talking Greek," my friend said.

"Yeah, the safest," I said, but not to take a risk? Not to take a move? Was that the best?"

"Yes, we should play it safe," my comrade said.

Thoughts rolled over in my mind as I waited in the silence looking at myself and my friend as we were there trapped like rabbits.

Then, we heard a sound.

"What's that?" I said.

"Nothing, maybe the wind is dropping," my friend said.

Then I lost my patience. 'The heck with the ifs and buts and maybes,' I thought. I wanted to find out what was going on.

Crawling, still hiding inside the bushes I made my way uphill, up and up until I got up on the top of the ravine. Looking around through my binoculars that I happened to carry, I couldn't see anybody, German or Greek. Although there was dead silence, the country side looked... different. It had a hopeful look in the grey of the grass of the dark winter shades, like foretelling of brilliant blues and hues of the coming spring.

That could not be. It was still winter.

Maybe the countryside reflected my sentiments, my hopes my optimism for taking a risk... or maybe I was hallucinating. I looked through my binoculars again, and saw reality. I saw the country-side as it really was in the winter, in deep colours but dark and dreary, with dreary forms spreading and extending in every direction... without human figures anywhere. Gradually, I began to distinguish the real and the unreal through my binoculars. Someone was apparently crossing the hill nearby, moving as in mourning. The figure resembled my mother! It was my mother. I called to her and the minute she saw me, she collapsed. I ran to her, and she was unconscious. When she came around, she cried, saying, "You're alive, you're alive! And we were so worried after Styliano told us that you had some kind of war going on in the shack."

"And how did Styliano know? He would have been dead had he come to the shack," I said.

"Of course, he came to the shack," she replied.

"And is he still alive?" I asked curiously.

"Of course, he heard the shots from a safe distance and he turned back. Do you think he is stupid enough to have gone on?"

I looked at my mother blankly. 'The heck Basil with your agonies, risks, buts and ifs and all that philosophical rubbish that make the simple and the obvious seem complicated,' I thought.

"And why did the Germans come up to our shack?" I asked her, still gazing blankly at her.

"Oh, those stupid Germans on patrol! They were going to head for Tsoutsouros to change the guard, but they got lost and took the track leading up to the shack instead. They couldn't tell the difference between a road and a path," she said with a winning smile.

"If they didn't see us, why did they fire at us?" I asked.

"Probably they were scared. They probably thought you were waiting for them... that you knew their plans!" my mother answered with a grin.

## The Battle of the Pig

Once one group of underground forces invited my group to celebrate Easter in a ravine near the village Housaka. We Greeks celebrate Easter in the countryside with feasts. It's like celebrating the rebirth of nature after a dreary winter. For that we would barbecue lambs on open spits.

That Easter, everybody brought lambs except my friend Manolis, who instead brought along a pig and a wooden box full of honey, about five kilos.

"What's the honey for?" I asked him, "It's not for the Germans, I suppose, to give them a sweat treatment."

"No, it's for my pig," Manolis said seriously, "While I'm turning the pig over the fire I'm going to splash it with honey to make it taste delicious."

"You're out of your mind. You only need spices and salt to bring out the flavor," I said, "You don't know what you're talking about."

"This is part of my secret recipe," he said, as he prepared to cook the pig with the honey.

"Listen... I told you I know how to cook meat."

"Your mummy taught you?" he interrupted me.

I didn't pay any attention to his wise crack.

"Listen," I said, "It's a shame! You're going to ruin it. At least, cook it as it is and those of us who want honey on it, can put some."

But my friend was adamant. He skewered the pig on the spit and prepared to splash on lots of honey.

"Don't do that!"

"Yes, I will?"

"I told you, I know how to cook meat. I've been congratulated for my cooking before. Even Carta has congratulated me a hundred times," I said. He continued on rolling his pig in the spit and splashing it again and again... with honey.

I could not stand the scene of it. Then, I looked around, looking at my comrades, hoping they would take my side, but they stood in silence. They were just listening to the arguments but were not prepared to take any sides, probably... because they didn't know much about cooking!

I didn't want to spoil the day by arguing, so I sat silently and continued to cook my meat, while I watched him angrily, cooking his, splashing it with tons of honey and saying at the same time, "It's going to taste good," and I thought the whole time: 'what a waste!'

Finally the pig was ready.

We tried it and we spat it out. Now the silence ended. I didn't say, 'what a fool' or anything like that. Why spoil the day for something that was done? I just said, "Now if the Germans come, we only have to serve them with that pig... and they'll run for their lives."

### The Boy With the Rifle

The son of a friend of ours wanted to have a gun. Nobody wanted to give him one, so he decided to take the matters in his hands, to search and find a gun. After a long investigation he accomplished his aim: he found a rifle that had been hidden in an attic for two hundred years.

Hidden as it was for such a long time, the rifle was in a state of disintegration, but the boy didn't get discouraged, even when he tried it, when he pulled the trigger that is, and the bullet dropped to the ground like a stone; our boy found the solution: to tie strips of cloth around the barrel for security. Now he was ready for practice, but where? But this didn't discouraged him either, for he took the rifle over to their shack up on the mountains and hid it there for the time being.

The father would never forget his boy's excitement as we asked him some day to come and help his father in making cheese in their shack, up on the mountains; not only that, the father would never forget his boy's enthusiasm when we saw Germans on our way up to the mountains. The boy said, looking at them, "I'll fix you up."

Then, the father felt obligated to calm the boy, saying, "Don't worry, my son, by the time you're old enough, we would have thrown the Germans out, so you would be able to live a better life."

But obviously the boy decided to be on the safe side: to practice and be ready. When we got to the shack and he found an opportunity to do so, he aimed first... at his coat hanging on the wall, and then he aimed outside the window.

Upon hearing the shots, we thought the Germans were coming back and ran inside to hide. Time passed on, but the Germans were nowhere. We could not explain from where the shots came from, neither the boy. He even tried to help us with our guesses.

Time went on with us preparing the milk to make cheese, and then, when we had to take the pot off the fire, it felt strange and heavier than usual, as if something was tumbling in it. We couldn't understand it.

"My Gosh, we wanted the milk to coagulate, but not this much!" we said. "What went wrong?" We tried to figure out.

Then, while we were cleaning the pot we found the culprit, the bullet. The bullet couldn't revolve in the broken barrel and instead it found refuge in the pot, after hitting the ceiling and bouncing back, dropping to the bottom of the pot... to be cooked away!

Now we understood everything... and so the boy...

## Runaway Horse

On one occasion I came down from the mountains and went to my house. I wasn't afraid to go home because all the local people were on the look-out for any German movements. No one was at my house.

But this time I couldn't find the key, and I decided to go to my sister Chrysis' house farther up the street. I went in and lay down on the bed to rest. I was relaxing, talking and joking with my sister and brother-in-law, a lightly built man, and I wasn't worried because I was sure that if any Germans were around, I would be notified by the people.

I had my gun with me, but as the belt was tight on my holster, I took it off. Suddenly, I heard a noise which sounded like horses, but my sister looking out of the door said, "They're Germans!" Then, my brother-in-law jumped up fast as if a horse had given him a big kick. He made straight for a hole on the wall of my sister's house, which connected hers to that of her neighbor.

"Come on, Basil. Follow me," he said, waving his hands frantically.

I looked at the hole. "I can't fit through that," I said, "I'll get stuck. With my big legs on one side and my head on the other I'll look just like a fish in a net-ready to be fished out by the Germans."

"Basil, your gun!" my sister whispered urgently and pointed to where it lay on the bed.

I picked it up and fumbling, I tried to hide it in my waistband. My brother's-in-law head appeared in the hole.

"Come on! What are you doing?" he said with a shrill voice.

"It's all right for you," I muttered under my breath, "built like a matchstick."

Then, I glanced through the half-open door, (We usually left the door open so that we could hear the signals) and I saw a German looking for somewhere to hitch his horse. The horse was heaving wildly, its hooves pounding on the cobble stones and the German looking impatient trying to tie up his horse.

Like a propeller of a plane firing into operation, I squeezed through the hole pushing with all my might, and there I was, behind my brother-in-law. Sitting on the floor in front of us were some old women weaving baskets.

"Be careful Basil, jump over them," he said, as we jumped over the women which made them draw back in shock, making room for our flying bodies. I remember hearing them say in startled voices,

"My son, my son... son, what are you doing? Where are you going? What's the matter with you? Are you going nuts? Everybody is going nuts nowadays."

I looked around the house. My brother-in-law, after gesturing to me to follow him, had disappeared. I was shocked and didn't know what to do, whether to hide there or go out in the open and disappear.

Meanwhile the women kept shaking their heads back and forth rolling their eyes and kept saying while they saw me pacing back and forth, "My son, my son... son, what are you doing? Where are you going? Are you playing games?"

'Yes... deadly games, indeed,' I thought.

I went outside the house looking carefully, moving very slowly, looking for any Germans that might have hidden nearby. I moved cautiously and the passersby looked at me suspiciously, their eyes bulging, as I bent and contorted my body so as not to be exposed to any Germans' view.

I ignored the people's curious expressions and went on as fast as I could until I reached the cover of our church. From there I could glance back towards my house. There were still the Germans on their horses going back and forth while the rider with the wild one was still trying to calm it, and that was probably the reason he went to my sister's house.

I wondered if they were really looking for me, but I couldn't risk going out into the open. The Germans could easily chase me and capture me. I figured that those riders could capture me easily as they would be able to brush the area fast. Thus, I needed to find better cover where horses cannot go.

I looked around for a solution, a safe place, but there were only the surrounding village houses. The mountains seemed a great distance from me. I thought of the trees that are on the boarder line around our villages and I looked beside the houses where were some ancient olive trees protruding from the grove nearby.

That's it! I would hide in the olive grove. The horses would not be able to ride through those ancient trees which with their spreading dense trunks and low hanging branches would protect me. From there I could safely watch the action.

I wondered what happened to my sister. Was she still in the house? Did she have to escape the same way I did? Were the old ladies still muttering: What are you doing? Are you playing games? as they wove their baskets. I thought I could still hear their shrill voices trailing after me.

Also, I worried that the Germans might take my sister or other women as prisoners, and what would I do? I knew I had a machine gun about a kilometre away and with that I could fight four or five Germans, if I lay in ambush.

I wanted to fight them because this incident happened towards the end of the war, when we were winning and naturally here in Crete we were more assertive towards the Germans.

I kept looking at my house until I watched the Germans break down my front door, using a large stone. Apparently they were looking for me, but they soon came out and left without taking anybody with them.

Why I had not been warned by the local people about the coming of Germans? It was that this time the Germans coming straight from the Gestapo in Haraka, got lucky. Their wild goose chase - looking for the elusive Basil - was led by a galloping horse that took them through short cuts that they would not normally use, and they arrived in the village ahead of the message, 'Rams, rams.' Horses after all are faster than rams!

### The Surprise Encounter

At the time Carta escaped, some English officers left in my responsibility some things to keep and put in boxes. Among them was a bag of gold coins. The boxes were to be picked up by somebody from Heraklion who would give us the password 'Karacalos'.

Finally a person came saying the password but we disagreed on the means of delivery, and he refused to take them. As a solution I wrote to a friend in Heraklion, named Dimitris Daskalakis, to ask if he could think of a way to get the boxes through the German lines inspecting the areas. I sent one of our news carriers to get the reply. My friend replied to me that the best way to transport the boxes was to put them in the middle of two big sacks filled with grain.

We loaded the boxes on our animals and we set to go at night. It was very dark. Only some sheer light of the moon penetrated the night. We were going through the rough countryside, passing different paths and streams. While we were passing a stream, we saw some threatening shadows coming down on us in the same direction. We thought they were Germans. Right away I told the others to stop for cover and for me to lurch ahead and find a spot from where I could be in a position for ambush. I figured those Germans might have been the German beggars who were not dangerous. We thought we saw them coming down on us, but actually they didn't, only for fifty to a hundred meters they did, and then they turned to the left. In other words they deviated from the main road and instead they turned left towards a small path. That path was unimportant, only we Greeks would have used it; it wasn't usual for Germans to use.

Then I figured those people we thought were Germans must be Greeks looking for dirty business. In this case, they were the ones who wandered around at night stealing animals from farms. I was beginning to feel frustrated and betrayed. Yes, betrayed, for the reason that so many people were sacrificing for their country and ideals and those scabs to betray our cause.

Getting mad, I lurched ahead approaching them. "Stop! You thieves! All of us are sacrificing for our country and you take advantage of us? You are only concerned with the needs of your meager, miserable selves!" I said.

I approached them more and more and with them retreating, shrinking more and more, until with fear in their eyes... they pointed their guns at me, telling me not to get any closer... telling me, "Stop, stop, we'll shoot!"

I thought: 'Would you retreat like a frightened animal giving them the satisfaction of having control, Basil?'

"Yes, scabs shoot! Will you go that far?" I said, still mad.

At this moment, one of them recognized me and shouted at them, "Stop the nonsense. This is Basil! Stop!"

They did. Out of shame or fear they listened to him, and out they went with me shouting after them, "You traitors! Don't you dare do it again. If I'll catch you again, I'll hang you!"

### The Mistaken Victim

One time, the Germans blockaded the village Skina. They moved fast into the area. The villagers were ordered to stay in their houses, but the people had been notified beforehand and all the men managed to flee except for one. Angrily the Germans crashed through the village, chasing the poor man who had been left behind. They shot at him but missed - by mistake a German was killed. As he lay on the ground a chorus of women gathered around him. "Did you see, that the Germans missed their target? They killed a German instead of a Greek!" the women of the village said one to another. "They're so angry! Now look at them, shooting and gesturing, and going back and forth looking for excuses. They're looking for a scape-goat. They would go after anybody."

"The Germans will retaliate. Yes, they'll retaliate," a chorus of women cried in desperation.

"Let's do something about it," said Sophia, a tall and slender young woman - she had studied to be a teacher.

"What can we do," another voice asked, "go and give our condolences to pacify them? If we go near the Germans not only might threaten us, but also might kill us."

"That's it," Sophia said, with a spark of inspiration. "We've got to give them our condolences."

"What are you talking about? Actually going down there, and how can we - we don't speak German anyhow - say: "my condolences for your German, sorry. Our men shouldn't have fled and they should have stayed to be killed by you, so you wouldn't have to kill one of your own."

"We don't know the German language or any other language," some women said.

"How can we do it? By gestures? Can gestures make a language?" a girl from the chorus said.

"Yes, we can make a sign language," Rosa, a plump girl with piercing eyes, said.

"And we know sign language," Sofia said, in a slow manner like she was deep in her thoughts.

"What do you mean sign language? Do you mean instead of talking we can just move our bodies in mournful manner and express our condolences," a girl said.

"It's not a bad idea, maybe that will pacify the Germans when they see us move in a peculiar way with sad faces," said Sofia.

"Like maybe dancing...' that would make them forget for sure," bursted Rosa.

"And kill us for sure," a woman from the chorus said.

"And miss the dancing?" said Rosa with a grin.

"Oh! Cut it out, the big jokes. Shame on you," said Maria, an older woman in black.

"We don't need any dancing or posing to pacify them, we need to impress them differently. With some short of a play, a sad parade maybe," Sophia said.

"How can you think of a parade even a sad one, at a time like this," Maria snapped back.

"Why not a sad parade like one we would have at a funeral. It can be a sad play. We would wear black and say 'mirologia' (mourning tunes), for instance," Sophia responded.

"Then, let's just arrange a funeral!" said some voices of another group of women standing by.

"That's it, a funeral," said Sofia, decisively. "We are going to hold a funeral for the German. We are going to impress them with such sad play that they're going to forget the mishap. Listen girls you're going to be dressed in your best black, bring the most colourful flowers and with the whole ritual we're going to impress them."

"And do you think the Germans are going to buy this?" Maria snapped back.

"Of course, it will be convincing. With our rituals and with our best voices it would be our way of expressing condolences," Sophia said.

"Appearances - appearances. The Germans are so angry, how can we really convince them that we are really sorry?" Maria replied.

"You said it, Maria - appearances, but you didn't say if we can make the right appearances. Isn't it what we all like, to make good appearances for sympathy and hear flattering statements to a point to overlook other things? The Germans are no different," Sophia said soberly.

"Oh! That's why in all funerals we hear about good deeds of the deceased..." said Eleni, a young girl of fifteen.

"Yeah! You learn as you grow up, Eleni," said Sophia.

"Don't we all? Imagine, in my old age to hold a funeral for an enemy and having to mourn him. How about that?" Maria snapped.

"So, it's decided then, we'll hold a funeral," Sophia said, "or does anybody have any other idea?"

"Oh! stop all this talking, Sophia, and get down to work to make the Germans buy our idea, and they wouldn't come after us in retaliation," a chorus of impatient women answered.

And that's how it was. A series of procession of women in slow march, holding bright flowers, each woman wearing a mourning Greek mask for the Germans to see and to be appeased... and they were as they saw the women tossing flowers on the German, saying 'mirologia' gesturing sad goodbyes while bearing him. The Germans didn't retaliate.

## The Guide Manolio

One of the very good guides in Crete was my friend Manolio Bisberakis. He was one of the best and fastest couriers we had. This was hard to believe by looking at him, for he was very short, plain and bland. He appeared not to measure up to anything, but he did. He had a remarkable physical endurance. During our expeditions he would walk for days without food. He could run fast as anybody could. He also had the peculiar disposition to be able to walk for three days without sleep and then to sleep for another three days in a row to make up.

He knew all the underground leaders, where they were, and how to get from one to another. He knew so much that once when caught by Germans, the guerilla leaders changed their hideouts for fear that Manolio would reveal their whereabouts under pressure of torture.

The Germans caught him in Amari, in the vicinity of the city Rethymno, where a lot of underground activity was taking place. They found out about resistance activities there and blockaded the area. He was accompanying some Englishmen and their translator Souris. They were in possession of a radio transmitter, which the

Germans wanted to seize. With hearing the code-signal 'Rams' everybody hid except Manolio who stayed behind to conceal the radio transmitter. But in doing so he was not able to get away and was apprehended by the Germans.

They tortured him to make him tell on us, but Manolio endured. He would say: "I'm only an errand boy. I just do household chores for them."

The Germans said, "if you see the people who get in touch with the English, would you identify them to us?" Manolio said he would. Then the Germans blockaded the nearby villages one at a time and ordered Manolio to identify people.

A method used by the Germans was to go into a village and order the villagers to gather in one place. Whoever was found in hiding would be executed on the spot, they threatened. Manolio was then ordered to observe all the people and point out those he knew. Manolio would not admit to knowing anyone, although in reality he knew many.

Another time, as the Germans were taking him to a village upon the mountains where he had to identify people, he told them that he knew a better way to get there – and indeed he did – better for the villagers that is, but not for the Germans. He led them through difficult areas and took them in circles forcing them to spend the night outside and only reaching the village at morning. This was to allow the villagers to see them coming and hide before the Germans blockaded the area. And that's what happened, only, when the Germans reached their destination and saw no people they got angry and beat Manolio almost to death.

Later, the Germans, tired and weary with being led on a wild goose chase, found a spot to lie down and sleep. Manolio seeing them asleep, thought that it would be a perfect time to escape. As he was getting up a German next to him awoke and pointed his weapon at Manolio and stopped him. Then the German laid his head down, using Manolio's feet as a pillow and Manolio's escape attempt failed.

When the Germans awoke, they found seven or eight donkeys which they took for transportation to the next village. They also found a donkey for Manolio to ride. The donkey they gave to Manolio was young and could run faster than the others, and pretty soon was ahead of them all. In doing that... probably the donkey figured, that he could outsmart them all, for he was braying so hard while lurching ahead that the countryside echoed with a deafening sound. "Wait a minute my donkey. You are my savior," Manolio thought. Then, Manolio glanced back, and saw the German who was supposed to guard him, to put his finger on his ear with a grimace that showed his displeasure of hearing the echo sounds.

'Ha, Ha,' Manolio thought, 'let's dupe the German behind, into that deafening business with the donkey while I'm advancing ahead... Yeah, like having a shouting match between echoes.'

Manolio turned addressing the German, "You... name, name?"

"Ono, Ono," answered the German.

"Ono, Ono, repeated Manolio, stressing his voice.

"Ono, Ono," echoed the countryside.

"Ono, Ono," screamed Manolio, while he was pinching the donkey making him run faster and bray louder and leaving the German further and further behind... until the German pointed his gun at him, and Manolio releasing his pinch and the donkey going slower uphill downhill and Manolio resuming the normal game of echoes.

"Ono, Ono," Manolio.

"Ono, Ono," the countryside.

"Grr, Grr", but it wasn't the donkey, it was Manolio mimicking the donkey, and then the donkey completing the deafening braying... and the German impatiently, irritably with one finger on his ear and the other on his gun saying, "Stop! Stop!"

Now pandemonium had erupted.

Manolio: "Grrr, grrr."

Donkey: "Grrr, grrr."

German: "Stop, stop!"

Other Germans further back: "Ha! Ha! Ha!"

Countryside echoes: "Ha, Ha."

Bedlam reigned. A chorus of voices and sounds, reverberations of laughs echoing off rocks, until... a sharp turn that Manolio knew too well... Suddenly, he jumped from his donkey and away he scuppered and disappeared.

The silence was Manolio's last laugh.

I can't describe the joy we all felt when we saw him return to our base in the mountains; the minute we saw him we jumped in the air. It was almost impossible to believe he was home again. Manolio even carried a German uniform with him. The uniforms were useful to us when we had to walk long distances and didn't want people to talk even out of enthusiasm perhaps - about seeing resistance fighters, for the wrong people might hear and tell the Germans.

Manolio not only had physical endurance, but also a sense of humour; for example, he really acted the part well of being a German, especially in German uniform. On our journeys he would go ahead where necessary to frighten locals to keep a distance so they wouldn't have time to recognize us.

While returning from a secret mission to meet a boat from the Middle East, and taking our route back to our base we had to pass fields where sheep were grazing. Unfortunately, we were spotted by sheepdogs whose barking attracted some shepherds. As they hurried closer to see what the matter was, I stepped forward.

"Basil step back, they might recognize you," Manolio shouted. With his hands waving in military salute, touching his German helmet, he said purposely, "After all I'm the commander here."

Then, he stepped in front of me and with his body erect he shouted in German, "Get lost," for the shepherds to be out of the way. They did. We saw their figures retreating behind the bushes, and behind some large stones.

We continued on ready to pass a hill top when behind a big rock we saw a head popped out and we heard a screeching voice carrying sounds of complain and disappointment.

"Are you hiding us from us, Basil! Shame on you. Did you pass us for Gestabite traitors? Shame, shame!

When I heard that I felt so bad that I thought, 'Is it worth it to be overcautious all the time? Is that a guarantee of making us feel secure all the time?' I didn't know the answer, but I knew I had to make an adjustment. I went back to my friends and apologized for not showing consideration and respect for their feelings.

Manolio accomplished so much for the resistance that the allied headquarters requested for him to go to the Middle East, to present him to the soldiers there for an inspiration and an example. They wanted him to tell the soldiers there about his deeds and give them courage. He didn't want to go, although we wanted him to, because it wasn't safe for him to stay here anymore. He had already escaped from the Germans twice and consequently they were on the lookout for him. In their search, the Germans got so disillusioned with him that they had listed him as a common criminal, a con man, for the people to watch out. The Germans would proclaim: "He is very dangerous, even though you wouldn't believe that he measures up that way. You should be aware of him. He is a con man!"

No matter how much we insisted for him to go, we could not change his mind.

"Why should I go there for them to see me and be disappointed when they see how I look? Let them admire me from afar, it's better."

"Eh, Manolio wants to look like Humphrey Bogart, in order to go there. You'll just have to wear your hat this way and that way, and you will look like Bogart" we would tell him, playing with his German hat, showing him, but to no avail.

"Bogart or no Bogart, I'm staying here in these mountains I know," he would say.

"And loose all that glory of inspecting soldiers and tell them whatever you want, and have them listen to you?"

"That's why I don't want to go, I don't want to fool them."

"But you fooled the Germans!"

"That was their prerogative!"

And so on.

On a mission when the Italian General Carta left for the Middle East, the people who were not able to get on the boat at that time, went with Manolio to another place to meet the boat later. On their way, early in the morning, they encountered a German blockade. They were informed on time of the blockade, and a number of those people were able to get away. They could not find Manolio because he was asleep in one place they hadn't seen. Since he was sleeping heavily in an isolated spot, he remained inside the blockade. When he saw Germans, he was able to get away again, but he was shot in the legs.

Even wounded he was still able to get away safely. He went to see a doctor for his wounds.

"Eh! doctor, the Germans sent me to you to take care my wounds," he said with his sense of humor.

They sent him to the right place alright. The doctor or someone else informed the Germans - maybe out of fear because Manolio was sought by the Germans so intensively - I don't know. The Germans came and killed him... finally... outrageous.

## THE AMERICAN

During 1944, while the allied forces were attacking the German lines more intensively, we for our part, were also doing more missions. On the boat from the Middle East every month or every forty days, we received more supplies of weapons and explosives. Also there were people coming from and going to the Middle East.

We had a very important secret mission involving commandos on the tenth of June, 1944. The plan was for the commandos to come to Crete for a big sabotage mission on a major German base. The English told me not to tell anyone, not even my co-fighters. The English were afraid that the secret mission would become known and word would spread before the commandos reached their destination. They believed this because the allies were winning, and the people here were expecting the allied forces to come and liberate Crete. They feared that islanders would be unable to keep the commandos coming a secret as they would think the commandos were the advance guard of the liberation force, and in their joy they would want to spread the good news. Thus, I agreed not to tell anybody, not even my shepherds who used to clear up our tracks the morning after.

On the day the torpedo boat was due, the English and I went down to the beach to get the commandos. There was a very rough sea and the torpedo boat could not reach the coastline long enough for all the commandos to get out. On the other hand, they could not give any signals for fear of the Germans seeing them. There was a second torpedo boat, and we thought that it had vanished. Thus, not all the commandos landed.

From there under the shadows of the nearby German outposts, carrying explosives, we set out for our destination. After a long trek through rough mountainside, climbing over abysses and crevices, slithering across rock screes, we had to stop for rest near the village Melithochori. I had already sent a friend to notify the people to provide us with whatever we needed for the rest of the way, for example, fresh animals and guides or to bring us food.

We settled in a cave on a heavily wooded mountainside, that was covered with mist, but I didn't stay because I had to meet our guides with their animals.

I returned when the mist had cleared away and the stars were out. I found the others outside the cave. They were all together having what seemed to be a feast. They were around a fire cooking meat.

I stood there and breathed in the smells, the odours of tobacco and charcoal mixed with the smell of the meat, garlic and herbs. But I stood on one side from these enticing smells preferring to breath the clear air of the mountains that was heavy with the scent of the trees. I was tired and the grass in the meadows made me want to lie down and rest.

I was almost asleep when one of the commandos leaned over me saying, "Come on, get up and look around. See what we got."

I got up and looked around. There were cheeses and meat enough for thirty people double of what we were. A commando said, "Now we shall have the strength to go, not just to the Middle East but to Egypt and back!"

After we had rested we went on, passing the place Pirouni, and then we reached our destination, Siva Malevisiou, where the Germans had their base.

Finally we arrived ready for action. We approached the base in groups. Tom Dobadin, with some others, preceded us, and somebody from the resistance forces there - his name was Giakoumakis - led us to the spot where we were to begin our operations. The spot was behind a makeshift wall covered with wild fig trees, which was just across from the Germans. We lay on the ground and stayed motionless until all our groups came up.

Like snakes we glided through the night. Each group had to follow their own plan. The plans were like a spiders web, converging on the target. We could not stray from it one inch. Even if we had to urinate it had to be on that spot. All the commandos had to be in position so we could hit the base at the same time, twelve o'clock at night. Surprise was our strength.

First, the commandos had to cut the wires that surrounded the German base. The wires had many rows of empty cans tied on them to make a noise if anyone touched them. We had with us time bombs so the commandos could blow up the barrels of fuel that the Germans, according to our information, had put them in huge underground tunnels covered with grass and trees. The commandos divided the explosives, oriented themselves to the base, and decided the direction they would take to set the explosives. As they talked, one of us who went to explore the area came back to say that the Germans also had watch-dogs and that they set them free at night.

There was dead silence, no one knew what to say. Then, the leader of the commandos, an Englishman, made a gesture with his machine gun and the translator explained to us that we had to go ahead according to our plans, no matter what we encountered. I, along with some other fellow rebels, stayed back from the wires about two hundred meters, for if one of us Greeks got killed and the Germans found the body in the morning, they would have killed local people and burned whole villages in retaliation. With the foreign commandos doing the sabotage, it was different. There was international law against holding the local population responsible for actions done by foreign saboteurs.

I, along with two other Greeks, Rizopoulos and Giakoumakis, stood in apprehension outside the wires, holding our breath straining for the slightest sound. Then I heard a sound like 'gree-gree', then I recognized the sound of English machine guns. Since the saboteurs had killed two guards and also cut the wires at the same time, the Germans got hold that something was going on and with their sirens full blast, they shot at random everywhere in the dark.

After some agonizing minutes, our comrades returned, running quickly through the night. We all wanted to get away fast, but one group was missing. We waited; still no sign of them. The Germans were now scouring the area, but we couldn't leave. Then there was a soft sound and a whistle. The other group arrived - at last. Everything had worked like clockwork as we had meticulously planned. We hadn't run far when the explosions started. The noise was deafening as explosion after explosion rocked the earth. The ground trembled beneath us as thousands and thousands of barrels of fuel burned.

We all returned to our base safely in Housaka, and later the commandos left for the Middle East.

When the commandos for the Siva mission came, we expected them to be English or Greeks as at other times. But on our way to our destination I heard one of them speaking English in a way I was not used to hearing. I listened and watched him more closely. He didn't look English either. He looked more like us Greeks, as he was tall and darker than the Englishmen, with an almost swarthy, expressive face. He had an aura of distinction about him in his manners. Furthermore, whereas the English would approach anything with a refined, deliberate manner, he would approach it with a relaxed down to earth attitude. Because of his quaint American ways and totally relaxed attitude, Bill – I prefer to call him by his first name – became known to us as the 'Americano'.

While unloading the boat and dividing explosives and equipment and taking them to various hideouts with our animals, I often noticed the American watching me. All must have been new to him, because I would catch his eyes on me any time I was commanding my people, or my guides. Bill would observe all these with thoughtful glances of curiosity and I could sense his approval. The Americano and I communicated with my broken English, along with glances, and gestures which marked the beginning of our long friendship which grew throughout the resistance.

Perhaps he valued my services and my command of my own people, for thirty or forty days later he came to my village to see me and ask for my assistance. I was to help him in his mission, which was to demoralize and weaken the German forces, by recruiting German soldiers who were dissatisfied with the Nazis.

He wanted me to find a string of agents and establish in the villages a network of people who would help him locate and assist Germans who were willing to defect. He said that he hadn't accomplished anything in the last month or so and that he needed to have a translator with him all the time. I told him that I had to get permission of the English and especially that of Alexis Render, the English officer who was cooperating with the missions at that time.

We went to the English who agreed in helping if I keep up with my missions. I cannot forget something else that Render said. With a fatherly smile he expressed: "Now I know that you're going to grow close to the Americano because Americans are as soft hearted as you are."

Next we went to my house in Fabriana to eat dinner. As we prepared to leave, I saw him fill his bag excessively with things.

"Eh, Americano, you don't need to take food with you. Our people offer food to any 'xenos' who comes to visit. It would be considered an insult if the 'xenos' refused to accept whatever was offered. Pack only some shirts and underwear... "Eh, wait a minute, you have to look like us… here is a jacket, see how soft it is," I said pointing to it. "It's made from sheep, you see. And here's a 'sariki' (headband) to put on so you will look like us Greeks and not so Americano."

And he did look like us. The jacket and the headband gave him such a Cretan appearance that he made a joke out of it.

"Basil, are you trying to baptize me?" he said, his face lit up as he glanced at me.

"We already did my friend by calling you Americano. Eh, Americano, you're part of us, now," I quickly replied.

Next, I gave him a bag 'vourlia' that we shepherds carry on our chests, to put his things in, but he looked so bewildered and fiddled with it in trying to put his things in it that I couldn't help thinking, 'why it is so hard to put a bag on. He looks so helpless like he never saw a bag before and he comes from America, land of plenty of everything including bags. Doesn't he know what a bag is?'

"Come on Americano, what's wrong with carrying a bag?" I said.

Bill smiled and relaxed a little. I tried to help him. As I lifted the bag, it felt heavy. I thought it only contained clothes, but as I felt a large lump I realized that the bag had coins in it, probably gold. Our eyes met and in that glance my thoughts were confirmed. I didn't say anything to Bill or anyone else about the bag except a couple of people I trusted to keep a particular eye on the bag wherever we went.

With our first stop at Ligokino I discovered that a group of resistance fighters were there and planned to hit the German station and take the grain that the Germans had gathered from the people's farms.

We had to solve the problem before confusion ensued. In an event of a clash between local resistance fighters and Germans the Germans would blockade a wide area threatening our important operation and set back our mission for a long while. We talked to our fellow rebels about which of the two operations should be carried out bearing in mind the long-term impact on our common fight for freedom. It was agreed that our plan was more important. They even offered to assist us by giving us an organizational map of the area and some people to help us.

It was not long after that we made contact with the first German who wanted to defect. He explained at length his situation and that of the Germans to Bill, who spoke fluent German. Bill told the German to go back to his station and bring any others who were willing to defect. He would only let the Germans go back to their bases if he was convinced that they could be trusted. As he formed his opinion about possible German defectors Bill relied on my response and my judgement. If I said the German could be trusted Bill would send them back; otherwise, we would take them away with us.

By this time Bill and I had formed a strong friendship despite the differences in our backgrounds and our lack of common language. Our strengthened friendship made us feel as though the two of us could free all of Crete together. I remember that often after we had worked hard and long and a mission was successful that we would look at each other, cheer, and wave our hands in the air.

"Basil, we're doing alright, we're going to Heraklion, to Hania, to Africa, to finish our missions and then America, America!"

Shortly afterwards, we went on to another village. There Bill tried to persuade me to take and look after his gold, but I could not understand him and I asked the translator to explain to me.

"No, no!" Bill interrupted, taking some coins and putting them in my pocket.

Then I understood that he didn't want anybody to know that I was to take care of his money. I learned later that Bill had money in order to pay people for favours or to buy food. Little did he know then that my country people would not only give us anything they had, but also they would fully cooperate with us to make the resistance effective without the lure of gold.

One time two Germans came to my village from Mesochori, saying they had friends who also want to desert their army, but as they had already spent several days in our village, we didn't send them back to their base right away for their protection as they had surely been missed by now. Bill composed a letter which they signed urging their friends to desert and come to us.

"Basil, they're good," Bill said, almost singing.

I gave the letter to a man named Stavrides and gave him careful instructions as to how he should deliver the letter to the Germans. Stavrides sent somebody else to do the job who wasn't instructed well enough, and instead of giving it to one of the two Germans, he gave the letter to their Greek cleaning lady named Katina who didn't give the letter to the men in person, probably she was afraid, but left it on one of the men's beds. As that room was shared by other soldiers, they found out what was going on, arrested the dissatisfied Germans and sent them away, probably for execution.

This incident alarmed the Germans. From then on and in light of a similar incident they even began to guard their own troops. In another case we gave a man named Zachariadis a letter to give to a would-be German defector. Usually we told the German simply to follow the person who had given it to him, but in this particular letter we told the German to try and take with him some items, such as small guns or binoculars.

He did so, but the guard he passed became suspicious of his actions and searched him. The letter was found and the defector made to talk. Then they went after Zachariades who made the mistake of not coming to me to hide but went to another village. The Germans got hold of him along with his brother and other relatives and after torturing them, they killed them.

But these incidents didn't stop us. We continued to enlist dissatisfied Germans because Bill was well organized and spoke German so fluently that he could really relate to and understand their character as to convince them to come to our side, relying on my opinion, too. He would say sometimes, "Basil, despite the difficulties, you and your people are doing a great job."

And even sometimes, when he would become enthusiastic, he would say again and again, "Basil, we're doing alright... we're going to Africa sometime, and then America... America!"

## Beginning of the End

The German massacre and burning of the village of Anogia in early winter 1944 in revenge for a successful resistance action had a big impact on our operation. German troops were moved to different places in order to surround the west side of the Psyloriti Mountain and blockade the neighbouring villages. With the movement of the troops, our operations slowed because our agents had to establish different communications means in new areas, in order to find and approach the dissatisfied Germans.

In the meantime I went back to my base because it was a period of increased activity with my other missions. It was 1944 when the allied effort intensified on all fronts. We received more loads of weapons and had to distribute them to different groups of the underground forces.

I sent the American to a different territory to work after giving him a translator and organized another group of agents to help him. But to my surprise he came back some days later looking tense and lonely.

"You know Basil, I can't stay where you sent me. It's not the same as working with you in this area," he said, fixing his eyes on me, his face sombre. "I want to stay here and share the danger with you." I was pleased, to tell you the truth I had missed him too.

At this time an Italian agent of ours in the Gestapo sent us information that Germans were planning to blockade and search for underground activity in the Demati, Favriana and Kasteliana villages, along with the surrounding areas.

We were worried. It was winter and the earth being rough and bare would not hide our footprints and discarded objects from the Germans. However, as in the past the elements of nature had helped us to cover up our tracks, and so this time. We sent goats loose to eat from the trails and as they grazed they erased or covered up whatever marks or objects had been left on the ground.

In the mountains that the Germans were searching, we had caches of weapons and explosives. To avoid discovery we moved them into the plains. The fields now the open plains could not be as suspect as the mountains for concealing guerilla movements for the reason also we had the cooperation of the people in warning us and covering for any upcoming Germans. Thus, we operated this way for a time under the shadows of Germans, in the plains without any suspicion.

Meanwhile, as the weapons were being moved, Bill, the American, and I were near the village of Demati where we saw German troops go by. They had surrounded the area and captured some villagers and had already killed two people whom they found hiding. Somebody we knew from Demati who managed to get away told us what had happened and we were able to escape.

At this time, late 1944, the Germans were retreating on all fronts throughout Europe and Africa and becoming more desperate. The same was happening in Crete. Furthermore, the Cretan population, boosted by allied victories, showed greater resistance which provoked the desperate Germans to retaliate with more viciousness.

Times were very hard. They were blockading areas more often in their desperate attempt to supress the people. In the last blockades of the war two to three hundred people had been killed and an unknown number had been taken prisoners. In one search the

Germans captured eighteen people who had been in hiding and tortured them to make them inform on the resistance forces. I was amazed how these ordinary people endured that torture and never gave us away. Two of them were kicked to death. At the moment when the Germans were about to kill the remaining sixteen they received orders to take them to a concentration camp.

**The Sixteen Prisoners**

The Germans captured and put the sixteen people in the makeshift fence yard, out in a desolate portion of the country, by Demati. There they were inside the fence worrying about their fate, not knowing if they would be dead or alive the next morning. The Germans had actually planned to executed them the following day. Their plan was to call each man by name, ask him to step forward and then execute him. But a Greek translator, a patriot, warned the Greeks about the German plans.

"You guys, when you hear your names, pretend you're not there, don't step forward. keep calm."

Before the translator notified the prisoners, one of them, his name Vassilis, was so shaken and terrified that he couldn't even go to the bathroom. He tried and tried again and again in exasperation and disappointment saying, "I tried and tried but I can't pee. Nothing comes out. You think I was trying to lose my soul."

Dawn broke and the prisoners looked at the growing light with dread. A cock crowed and the birds began to sing in the villages as they were trying to transmit an optimistic message to the prisoners. Actually optimism was on the side of the Germans as they entered the compound with clean clothes, and after being well slept, and with such underlying energy that they barked at the prisoners and brought them to attention.

The men shuffled forwards silently staring into space like zombies. No one spoke. The commander unfolded a list while a firing squad stood nearby ready to unfold its lethal fire to put an end to life.

The German was reading the names, "Anthony Petrakis," he barked.

No one moved. The German called out other names but none responded. None showed even a flicker of recognition at his own name. They stood to attention playing dumb.

The German officer looked perplexed. He couldn't understand it; maybe playing dumb was contagious.

"These are not the right men," he snapped after reading the list.

Vassilis ran off quickly but not to escape from the Germans. He disappeared behind a tree. When he returned his grin was white.

"I didn't lose my soul, but I lost something else..." he said with relief.

In the meantime, because of the German blockades, my own and three other espionage groups - like the group of the Englishmen Render and a group of the Greek Thomas Temelaki - moved on the open plains, in order to execute operations speedily. We were not in the mountains and that was very dangerous because in the plains we were more exposed and could not hide as easily when danger loomed.

Thus, I called my friend Badouvas, a rebel in the mountains, but not involved in the missions or espionage, and asked him to take some of us into his area so that fewer of us would be exposed to danger and also to spare the population from possible German reprisals. Actually I had a hard time convincing him to go.

I told the American to go with Badouvas to another area where he could conduct his operations recruiting dissatisfied Germans more successfully.

As the end of the war drew near and activity on our part intensified we received more weapons from the Middle East and sent more people there. Consequently my work intensified: organizing missions, finding pack animals and local guides, and so on.

For espionage work I had to coordinate all our movements when we gathered information from all crucial spots such as the German nautical bases in order that the allied forces could come later and bombard the German bases right on target and at the right time. The allied forces needed to know every movement of the Germans, so that they could come and bombard the German installations.

The Germans tried to camouflage their movements by covering their war materials and by moving them from place to place but no matter how many times they hid their armaments or established new bases they were always found out by the local people, who would inform the resistance.

It was a day that I'll never forget as long as I live. We were down by the sea on one of our missions. It was late at night. Suddenly we heard unusual sounds, but not the threatening sounds we knew so well. Was it an animal? But what animal? We heard cracking twigs, breaking branches, slipping on stones in haste... Then out of the darkness with his face lit up, one of our couriers appears.

"Basil, Basil... the Germans..."

"What."

"The Germans are retreating..."

"Where?"

"Towards Heraklion."

"At last," everyone responds. Some shouted "Hurrah."

"Shhh, shhh, the Germans might hear." someone said.

"We're not afraid, at least we can go free." "Hurrah," all of us said, "Let's go."

We continued on. We wanted to go everywhere. The roads felt that they were opening up for us, taking us to a newly liberated area, to other villages, to celebrate.

Happy that we were being liberated, all of the rebels gathered in my village, to celebrate the retreat of the Germans with a feast; a feast I'll always remember. Our shouting echoed around the houses, our feet danced the streets and our bodies were warmed with a million hugs of delight.

We were in the village of Alagni celebrating when Bill came along with his translator Anthony Giamalakis and dragging along with him a young German who had recently decided to defect. Bill and I fell on each other hugging, throwing our headbands in the air, whooping with joy as if we hadn't seen each other for years not just fifteen days.

"We're free at last," we said to one another.

Our conversation was as rapid as machine gun fire. The German watched us puzzled and obviously curious about what we were saying. Anyway, during the course of our conversation Bill told me that he had learned from spies that the retreating Germans were planning to destroy the airport in Kastelli and we had to prevent it from happening.

"I'm going to seek the cooperation of everybody in the rebel forces, rightists or leftists, in order to save the airport," he said.

The German he had with him knew about the German installations around the airport and would help us find and cut the wires around it.

"We should not let the Germans in their desperation destroy the public facilities."

"Like extracting a price for something lost." I completed.

"We are not going to let them," Bill said.

Then, we started drawing up our plans of action.

## THE GERMAN RETREAT

With the Germans in retreat we needed to coordinate the activities of all the resistance groups. Bill had told me that he wanted to visit groups that had left-wing overtones, as well as those on the right. It has to be said that as the external threat of the Germans diminished, the political nature of the resistance groups came to the surface. I had friends in both camps, so I could help in the negotiations.

I took Bill to the captains of both factions of the resistance groups, first to the captains Badouvas and Plevris. They said they would help.

"Basil will get you in touch with other captains closer to Kastelli and we will give you a car to get there fast."

We left the car in the village of Meli, which was on the way and close to Arcadohori, the leftists' headquarters and Bill and I continued on foot to Arcadohori with Bill's companions.

High on the mountains behind the shadows of trees stood the leftists' headquarters. When we approached their camp, guards came out, at first apprehensively, but their faces lit with ease as soon as they recognised me.

"Eh, Basil, 'kalos orisate' (welcome)," they said, beaming.

Then the guards notified their leaders, George Papamastorakis and Michalis Samareitis, who came out to greet us. Their reception was friendly and Bill was pleased that they agreed to help us. Bill, even held my hand the whole time and said over and over, "good, good."

The captains took us to a car and drove us to the village of Aghia Paraskevi where we got out. We continued on foot through mountains to Kastamonitsa to meet friends who were in touch with the Germans. Our plan was to have them help us reach any army officers who were dissatisfied with the Nazis. We would try to bribe them not to destroy the airport or at least allow us to save it. The plan was that we would sneak into the airport at night and disconnect the wires that had been placed around it.

We met our friends in a place at Spyridiano. While we shared our plans the silence was split by a deafening noise. Explosions seemed to crack the sky with slices of fire. They were coming from the direction of Kastelli airfield. Apparently the Germans had begun to retreat from the area blowing up installations as they left.

Close to us were some young shepherds who were also watching the destruction. With a curiosity that characterizes youth their eyes continued to comb the area when one of them spotted a car far off in the distance. I heard him say, "It's a German car and it's coming towards us."

A thought raced through my mind. I remembered that Bill and I had talked about our need for a car and that we should seize one from the Germans. I grasped my machine gun and ran down to the road towards the bridge finding cover under a tree near it.

I heard my companions shout, "You're out of your mind. Come back."

I myself did not understand what was driving me on. Somehow instinctively I was forced forward into action. Even the pine needles, prickling my elbows where I lay under the trees, spurred me on. My friends didn't think the car was worth risking my life for, but having started I could only go on.

The situation was clearly dangerous for there could very well have been more than one car, but I was so focused on my target that I hadn't thought about that at that time.

As it neared me, I got up ready to force the car to stop and tell its two occupants to get out with their hands up. When it was almost level with me I stepped out just enough to be able to see it, shot four or five times and shouted, "Stop!"

The driver stopped, but one of the men jumped out and ran towards the bridge for cover. I shot at him and he fell. The other man got out of the car also and worked his way towards me pointing his gun. I crouched for cover but didn't want to shoot him; I wanted to take him prisoner. I waited but he shot at me, and I was forced to shoot back and hit him.

I shouted to my companions, who were above me at the top of the hill, asking if there were more Germans. There were none, and my companions came running down with huge strides, bounding over the earth, happy that I had survived. Bill was especially enthusiastic as he asked me if I was alright, his voice trembling. He said he would send a cable to the allied headquarters about what I had done.

Happy that I had survived, my friends had a party for me. They even made up a song for me in a hurry, with all the trimmings...

'He's a wonderful fellow, he's a wonderful fellow... that the birds even fly low to see him.' And so on. 'Ah, ah...'

Bill sang more with an even louder voice adding more lines.

"We're going to go to America...we're going to go to America..."

"Where everyone wants to go now," we responded.

Then, I would sing back, like in our 'mandinades', "Ah, ah, but let's go around all of Crete first..."

We didn't want to stop adding more words, and singing funny lines again... in response... It seemed to never end – to a point of absurdity.

We drove the car with the bodies of the Germans to Kastamonitsa where we hid the car and had the bodies disposed of so that the Germans wouldn't find and take revenge on the local people. In Kastamonitsa Bill typed fliers saying that the two Germans had defected to the allied forces and that civilians had not been involved in their defection. He also noted the necessary information from their I.D. cards.

We distributed the fliers throughout the recently evacuated Kastelli airfield. At the same time some of us went to the surrounding areas and hid in the valley of Lasithi in case the Germans made any reprisals. There was none, probably because their tanks had been withdrawn to Xida as they were in a hurry to retreat and leave Kastelli. I left Bill in Kastelli after I had put him in touch with people who would help him recruit dissatisfied Germans.

Everything was in a state of flux. It was anarchy. As the Germans retreated their command structure was diminishing and so did ours. On the Greek side political tensions came to the fore hampering successful clean-up operations. On the German side there was little or often-times no discipline, no structure. The whole situation was explosive, and as always when a system breaks down, irresponsible elements come to the surface. The ensued instability farther complicates any opportunities for political or civilian solutions.

With the breakdown of order many dissatisfied Germans felt justified to desert, which gave Bill a very busy task indeed. Bill had developed a basic technique in recruiting Germans. Our agents would look for dissatisfied Germans and contact Bill. He would talk to the person in fluent German, and try to convince him to come to our side. If the potential defector was skeptical about the safety of the action, Bill would give him a letter to use in case he decided to defect at a later time. He would be instructed to give the letter to any Greek citizen who would then lead the German to us. The letter read: "Greek patriot, you will do great service to your country if you lead this German soldier to our liberation forces."

Bill intensified his operations with the ultimate goal of speeding up the disintegration of the German forces in Crete, to force them to pull out faster. He set up headquarters in a village called Spilea. He had enough people working with him by now to set up a network in German camps to enlist German defectors.

His agents distributed persuasive notes, letters and fliers. Meetings were arranged with Germans in a health clinic named Mandalenis that we used for cover. In this way their comrades wouldn't be suspicious to see them going to a health clinic for treatment - but what a treatment! The right one of course. From there we channeled them to the Greek headquarters in Staihtades or Kastelli or to the English and Greek military division of the resistance.

For a while Bill, his translator and the German Loudovico, went to Peza to continue his operations. On their way they barely escaped a blockade and ran for their lives. If it wasn't for some local people who saw them at the last moment and gave warning they would probably have been killed. Later they said they were saved "by a miracle."

In the meantime, I was called by Tom Dobadin to Kali Kastelli to attend a meeting with some English military commanders from the Middle East. Its purpose was to decide how to take over Heraklion now that the Germans were retreating.

In these turbulent times Bill's translator, one of the most effective agents at enlisting Germans, was unfortunately caught by the Germans in a blockade. We tried to find some way to rescue him from a jail in Chania where he was held, but while we were arranging his escape, the Germans sent him elsewhere thwarting our plans.

At the same time as we were trying to find a way to save him we learned additional information that the Germans planned to cause serious damage to the infrastructure of Heraklion, to destroy its airport, sewer system and port.

As action had to be taken quickly, Bill, the sheriff of Heraklion Liapakis, and a bishop met in a restaurant. The meeting was not held clandestinely because time had begun to change; freedom of movement was a result of standing now on equal terms with our enemy. We had to decide what to do to save Heraklion's public facilities. On Bill's initiative, and with my approval, we decided to set up a meeting with the German commanding officer of Heraklion.

Bill wrote a letter requesting a meeting and proposing to negotiate reasonable terms which would be suitable to both sides. They were: to cancel the bombing of public facilities in exchange for Cretan cooperation during the German retreat, and return of Antoni Giamalaki, Bill's translator, in exchange for German prisoners we were holding. The commanding officer could choose the meeting place, bringing military protection if he wanted. Our commander, George delivered the letter by hand.

We were still at the restaurant not having finished our drinks when our commander returned with the reply which named the meeting place. Bill asked me to gather local men who would accompany us for protection. I was instructed to go ahead with them to the meeting place and also contacted some groups in the underground forces that had been ordered to the villa Ariadna by the English to watch the German movements. I did and on our way there, in Vanizeli, we met eight tanks full of Germans heading in the same direction.

The tanks, and the car carrying the commander and his adviser cut through throngs of people who were spreading in every direction, not knowing what was happening and afraid of a clash with the Germans. They tried to warn us but little did they know that it was prearranged and under our control. Of course, the Germans could have killed us all, but even within the chaos of war there are rules and regulations, and violence is not totally unrestrained.

In any event, I was busy observing German movements around us in case they had set a trap. Meanwhile we talked about the issues that concerned us all and ended up agreeing that the Germans would not bombard the public facilities, especially since Bill successfully argued that they didn't have any right to do so. We agreed to facilitate their evacuation by not launching an offensive against them during the retreat. They did not agree, however, to free Bill's translator for our German prisoners.

Because skirmishes with the Germans were occurring in the civilian sections of the cities, we decided at the meeting to define the area in which the Germans would be free to move during their withdrawal from Heraklion. In this way casualties on both sides could be kept to a minimum. After the meeting, the German commander left, but his advisor remained with us in order to implement our agreements immediately.

Holding my machine gun, I rode in the German car with the advisor followed by another car carrying the bishop and my comrade, Lafaki. Again if they had wanted to kill us nothing would have saved us as we were surrounded once again by Germans.

However, I felt safely guarded by the unwritten conventions and rules of the war which was coming to an end like a clock unwinding, to its final hour. I hadn't wanted the other car to follow as I felt safe, but one of my co-fighters, alert, his face tense, had jumped to my side, his finger on the trigger of his gun as he said with resolve, "I'm not going to leave you all by yourself, captain Basil," and he came with me.

We travelled to the German office at Heraklion and advised any troops we met to pull back behind the lines we had agreed. I did the same with any resistance force we met just as I had agreed at the meeting. To tell you the truth, I didn't know the area towards Heraklion in detail, but I followed the instructions Bill had given me.

In a few days the troops pulled back to their military camps in Heraklion and kept themselves there. With that the Cretans could finally move freely and celebrate their freedom with gusto. The scene in Heraklion was unforgettable. A river of people filled the streets hugging and kissing each other while the bells of every church rang out joyously - freedom was ours! Bill and I were swept along in the human current. The bells filled the air with the magnitude of our relief and happiness.

Bill and I searched out and found the German advisor of the military command and discussed with him the possibility of a treaty. The advisor said he didn't have the authority to do that, but he would take us to the commander. Bill arranged a committee composed of himself as the representative of the United States, George Generdos as a representative of the Greek forces, Nick Souris the English representative, and I was to represent the rebel forces. We were to meet the commander at the airport of Heraklion.

Once there we saw the German garrison getting ready to leave for Chania. The commander made us wait for more than an hour while he came from the camp. He had about him an air of hesitancy that was totally at odds with his strict military bearing, for he was obviously uncomfortable and reluctant to make any binding agreement with us. Bill proposed that the Germans capitulate and in exchange the resistance forces would not attack the Germans during the retreat.

In order to convince the commander, Bill warned that a German retreat to Hania would bring upon them a serious number of casualties because the local people and the rebel forces would attack them along the way. In spite of Bill's efforts, all arguments were to no avail. Following our unproductive meeting we went back to our group which the local Greek authorities had stationed in an apartment house in Heraklion, in Karteraki.

With our liberation in essence my mission and Bill's was finished. The time we had striven, worked and dreamed for had arrived, and soon Bill and I would have to part, perhaps for ever. I left with Bill to return to our base in the mountains. We rode back on a motorbike through the mountain trails like goats, bumping over crevices and jumping over the road's bends and switchbacks. As we climbed steadily higher, we felt the air colder and colder. Then our bike would descend abruptly laboring and tossing us from one side to another...

We had a hell of a good time. Yes, we had a good time, especially when both of us on and off our bike, we joked about our numerous operations, recruiting Germans from their army... stealing we called it.

We returned to our base safely. Soon afterwards it was time for Bill to leave. After he had gathered his possessions and finished writing his diary the sad day came for him to leave. It was the moment that deep inside ourselves we had dreaded, the point where the paths our lives took would separate. By a quirk of fate our lives had been thrown together and now we were going back to our own separate worlds, to our different worlds.

## The Parting

I cannot forget his tall distinguished silhouette against the Cretan sky, with his eyes capturing the surroundings, looking intensively as he tried to imprint into his mind every detail of the countryside he had known all this time he was there.

"Now that you became one of us you'll leave, Americano," I said empathetically

"No, Basil. I'm not really leaving. I'm taking with me all the memories to sustain me and remind me of how it was."

"And how it was, Americano?" I said with a smile as I wanted to extract from him his deepest thoughts. "Remember, we're going to conquer the world, starting with Heraklion, going to Egypt and then to America... so far we've only managed Heraklion," I said.

"We'll conquer the world alright," Bill said with a smile, "but first Crete, now it is free. I'll come back when Crete is completely rebuilt and free from the destruction of war. Then I will see the real beauty of it, and I would really get to know the people living their normal lives in their own way."

I laughed and said, "Once you've experienced Crete, its like tasting raki. You just have to come back for more."

Bill stepped forward, hugged and kissed me in the Greek way with valour. He picked up his 'vourlia' his shepherd bag, slung it as easily as a Cretan, saluted and walked away.

As the Germans retreated to Hania, they blew up bridges and roads behind them to prevent our attacks. All the public administration and local government was in a chaotic state with an ever growing possibility of a clash between the leftists and the rightists. I tried to mediate where I could as I was neutral and had friends on both sides.

We were in the process of making an agreement to establish a unified local authority. Of course, there were some irresponsible elements on both sides and unfortunately there was an attempt to kill the leader of the leftists, Podias, which stirred up passions. Bill was still in Crete and both of us intervened trying to calm the situation. Captain Badouvas took charge of arresting the criminal and a military court condemned him to death.

This was the most serious instance of disagreement, although there were some clashes stemming from new irresponsible elements. Most long-standing resistance fighters were conscious of their mission to serve their country and all the resistance groups participated in administrating the local government. We divided responsibilities. My group administered the port, Captain Badouvas commanded the countryside, and Captain Michalis Samaritis administrated the garrison commander's office. This situation continued until October 1945 and the communist insurgence on the mainland.

After the Germans left, everything was in ruins... roads, bridges, sewer systems, everything was either run down or destroyed, but thanks to the Marshall Aid Plan by which American money played a huge part in the post-war reconstruction of Europe, Greece started to rebuild.

I can add that women provided a base of support for us. Besides working in the fields and preparing food for us they spied on Germans and could watch their movements easier than men as they were not under as much suspicion, especially during critical times. Furthermore, women would transmit to us whatever they heard from other women who were supposedly friendly to Germans. Also the women gave letters to Germans willing to defect.

Some women even showed a passive resistance to German force or coercion. I can give an example. One night some Germans went to a village and asked its president for room and food. The president distributed the Germans to a few houses. One of those houses belonged to my cousin Irene.

Because members of her family had been killed by Germans, she refused to accommodate them when they got to her house, sat down at the table and demanded to be fed. Then Irene said with contempt, "No, no... I will not serve you murderers."

The Germans got up angrily making threatening and insulting gestures, but Irene kept saying, "I won't serve you murderers," as she was moving for cover until the Germans got the message she wasn't afraid.

On the other side of the table stood Irene's mother. The mother knew that she had to come up with something. The Germans were adamant and so was her daughter.

The mother looked at the pot of food she was holding. "Look, look," she pointed to the Germans, pushing the pot into their faces with the steam coming out clouding their vision.

Now Irene, pretending to get something, was backing up to the door, stepping out the door into the night, into a neighbor's house and from there to another village.

This time... it was dawn, the longest dawn as we sat finishing the story, reliving a long past, a harsh but dear past. It was almost dark. Basil's figure receding in the dark but his voice clear, resonant and unpretentious made him appear larger than life, a challenge to life.

We were engrossed. We didn't turn on the light, we felt as the room was filled with the people of the story... as the light might drive them away... drive away Bill, Tom, Leigh and Yiannis, George, Irene...

Suddenly, the door opens, and a silhouette glides in...

"It's getting dark... I'll turn on the light."

"My wife..." Basil said.

"You mentioned in the story about your friends who would tease you, about not being married, but you didn't mention anything about getting married..."

"With the events of the war you forgot to mention our wedding? It was a big event."

"No, I didn't... only so far. Who could forget. It was a big event at the heart of the war alright."

"My wife and I met during the resistance..."

Then, glancing at his watch Basil said, "...but this is for another time. Let me finish the story first."

In retrospect all these ordinary, poor or uneducated people unified in their cause and seeing liberty as their ultimate goal, contributed to the allied cause more than a whole army could. We watched the German movements, using radio transmitters and our own resourses. We were more useful to the allied forces than a whole army. With our 'wireless stations' we provided allied forces with information which enabled them to sabotage and attack German bases in the southern part of Greece. Our strength came from the fact that our people were united and supported the resistance to the point where families gave their own food or their children's food, to the resistance forces.

More than that, people often paid with their own lives for their passive resistance. Resistance thwarted German attempts to maintain law and order and forced them to keep more soldiers than were necessary on the island. In retaliation for anti-German activities the Germans would blockade areas, seize people and torture them to make them tell on us; nevertheless, the people chose to die rather than capitulate.

I can mention from my own family that my sister's father-in-law and one of my brothers-in-law were tortured and killed. Of my friends who were executed for the same reason were Dimitris Daskalakis, Antonis Fartaros and Raftopoulos Alexandros, who was one of the first in the resistance helping the refugees from the battle of Crete. There were many, many more who sacrificed their lives.

...and that's the way it was... or, how it is in life, at one time or another.

## EPILOGUE

### The Outrageous

Some years passed in peaceful life. All of us went back to work to bring order to the shambles war had left behind and to heal the scars. We went on as well as we could as before the war, but now, in our everyday civilian life, in our social gatherings, we would feel the load of contradictory emotions - the painful and pleasant, the outrageous and the normal, as they had been in the context of war.

But only the outrageous persisted to give us compensation for the pains we went through; for instance, when we gathered for feasts, we would clink our glasses, drink to health and sing our ballads, we would reminisce about outrageous incidents, such as 'The Pig'. My friends would reenact the whole scene, mimicking how I looked angry, ready to fight, as Manolis, unperturbed, cooked his pig with its spread of honey. Even now, when I see Manolis on the street, I greet him with our standard joke saying, "Remember the pig?"

### The Unexpected Striptease

One day I went to a coffee shop to meet some people I knew. The owner used to be the representative of our district, but to tell you the truth, he was quite conceited, and liked to brag about himself sometimes. As I entered the coffee shop, there he was, sitting with a large group of people. All of them listened, with wide eyes, enthralled as he told war stories and about his brave deeds. I was invited to join them, so I listened to his stories for a while.

Then, at some point, while he was boasting about something, I thought to myself, 'the truth must be told', and I said, "I admit that you're cool... but you forgot that one time I had you cornered, and you didn't know what to do, when I sent you to the Middle East with only your underwear on."

Hearing that, he got up and mumbled between the laughs of the others.

"Don't remind me of that, stupid fool. I didn't have any other choice."

Then, with less assurance he went on to explain how the people he was with in that boat got undressed too to give away their clothes, how they wrapped themselves in blankets in the cold and in the dark, and how many days they were without clothes until they arrived at their destination in the Middle East. From that time on his stories didn't have the same impact.

### The Surprise Meeting

My children grew up after the war and knew a peaceful life. One of my daughters worked as a receptionist at a major hotel in Crete. One day a visitor came to the hotel. He was a foreign officer who collaborated with us in the resistance, my daughter was told.

"You must have known my father from the resistance," she said.

"Who is your father?"

"Basil."

And then he answered, "Go and recite him the lines from the following song," and to my daughter's surprise, he actually sang some lines of a song we sang at one of our get-togethers in the mountains.

When my daughter told me, I ran impatiently to meet him, not for cover this time, but for uncover... to find out who he was.

There he was standing... his face away, but his voice echoing that warmth that I knew so well. It was Leigh Fermor.

"Basil!"... We hugged each other. "Do you remember, Basil, our good times in the war?" he said.

"Yes indeed... like that," I sang more lines of the song while the standing-by people's faces turned in bewilderment, ours in agreement. We continued the absurdity.

"And that was going on during the war? That's outrageous!" the voices of those standing by said in amazement.

A thought raced into my mind: 'War is outrageous, and whoever is involved in it becomes outrageous in one way or another.'

We continued reminiscing, and then Leigh asked, "Have you heard from Bill..? But this is another story.

## Author's Epilogue

As I travelled through the island, I was so impressed with its beauty, its majestic contrasts, its golden valleys, its picturesque villages and hospitable people, that I started taking notes of everything that amazed me.

Mingling with the people, being invited at events, I noticed again and again the people's closeness to the land, to the rocks and soil, and how it affected the roots of their society as it was expressed in their history, and in their legends.

"I will return. We will return," I told my daughters, and we would take a ride through the countryside again and especially through the mountains that sustained the resistance, and visit places to find out who came back after the war and how, to reminisce about the outrageous, the impossible and the normal during the war... or to tell about other adventures.

Above all, to visit the other places of Crete, the cities, the other towns, and the other villages. Then, we would get to know more about Crete and its beauty; its natural wonders, its people, and its legends...

"Even contemporary legends... like Basil's wedding - as I heard... or your wedding, mom," my oldest daughter said.

"What! My wedding!"

"No, it was just a slip of the tongue! I meant the one in which you were the koumbara... I'll always remember all the mishaps we had during that wedding and afterwards. Who could forget, especially when we tried to dance the pendozali like the Cretans, Ha! Ha!" she said.

"Oh boy! I'll have my camera ready next time, for sure," my youngest daughter said with a crafty grin.

# BIBLIOGRAPHY

Doren, David. **The Winds of Crete,** Athens:
Efstathiadis Group, 1981

Bowman, John. **Crete,** London:
Jonathan Cape Ltd, 1984

Drossos Bros. **Crete,** Crete:
Hraklion, Crete

Archer, R. **Crete,** Athens:
Efstathiadis Group

Hopkins, Adam. **Crete: Its Past, Present and People.** London:
Faber & Faber Lim, 1987